Grant Allen

Dumaresq's daughter

Vol. I

Grant Allen

Dumaresq's daughter
Vol. I

ISBN/EAN: 9783337040369

Printed in Europe, USA, Canada, Australia, Japan

Cover: Foto ©ninafisch / pixelio.de

More available books at **www.hansebooks.com**

DUMARESQ'S DAUGHTER

A Novel

BY

GRANT ALLEN

AUTHOR OF
'IN ALL SHADES,' 'THIS MORTAL COIL,' 'THE TENTS OF SHEM,' ETC.

IN THREE VOLUMES
VOL. I.

London
CHATTO & WINDUS, PICCADILLY
1891

CONTENTS OF VOL. I.

CHAPTER	PAGE
I. BY THE GATE OF THE SEA	1
II. LINNELL'S MYSTERIES	27
III. LOVE—THIRTY	46
IV. A PROPHET IS NOT WITHOUT HONOUR	69
V. A MODERN STOIC	95
VI. A SLIGHT MISUNDERSTANDING	120
VII. AT THE UNITED SERVICE	141
VIII. GETTING ON	165
IX. FOR STRATEGIC REASONS	181
X. AS BETWEEN GENTLEMEN	191
XI. FOOL'S PARADISE	204
XII. THE BUBBLE BURSTS	227

DUMARESQ'S DAUGHTER

CHAPTER I.

BY THE GATE OF THE SEA.

WHEN any man tells you he doesn't know Petherton Episcopi, you may immediately conceive a low opinion of his character and intellect. For all the world, in fact, has been to Petherton. Not, of course, in the same broad sense that all the world has been to Margate and Great Yarmouth; nor yet in the same narrow and restricted sense that all the world has been to Brighton and Scarborough. The vulgar mob that frequents the first, the fashionable mob that frequents the second, would find in Petherton nothing to satisfy their essentially similar and gregarious tastes. Birds of a feather flock together in the crowded promenades of the Spa and the Pierhead. But the quiet, cultivated, nature-loving few, the saving minority who form the salt of the earth (according to Matthew Arnold) in these latter hurrying scurrying centuries, all of them seem by some native instinct or elective affinity to have picked out the very name of Petherton from the list of competing English watering-places at the end of Bradshaw.

You have been there yourself, I feel sure beforehand, so I needn't describe it to you. It is of a type, indeed, with Lyme Regis, and Sherringham, and St. Ives, and Overstrand; with Newquay, and Aldeburgh, and Mundesley, and Budleigh Salterton; one of the many unspoilt nooks and corners in a broken gap of rockbound coast, shunned by the vast class of noisy tourists to whom the seaside means only a pier and an esplanade and a military band and a crowd of loungers—but dearly prized by simple old-fashioned souls, like you and me, to whom the seaside is synonymous rather with open cliffs and heather-clad heights and creeping surf and a broad beach, broken only by the fishermen's boats and the bare brown legs of the shrimpers in the foreground. Hence, when any man tells you he doesn't know Petherton, you may set him down at once with tolerable accuracy in your own mind as a son of the Philistines—a member of the Yarmouth and Scarborough contingent—and take his mental and moral gauge accordingly.

Charles Austen Linnell—he was careful to put the accent, himself, on the last syllable—found Petherton suit him to the very top of his liking. It lies surrounded, as you know, by high sloping hills, with a sea-front undesecrated as yet by the financial freaks of the speculative builder, and a tiny stone pier of Plantagenet antiquity, enclosing in its curve one of the quaintest and oldest coasting ports in all England. There are endless 'bits' to sketch in the neighbourhood; and Linnell, who loved to describe himself as 'a painter by trade,' found subjects ready to his hand at every turn of the picturesque old borough. He stood in front of his easel on the west cliff, that summer morning, gazing with ingenuous admiration and delight, first at the cottage with the creeper-covered porch, and then at his own clever counterfeit presentment of the same on the sheet of thick white Whatman's paper stretched out before him. And well he might; for it was a cottage of the almost obsolete poetic type, the thatched and gabled cottage with low overhanging eaves now being rapidly crowded out of existence in the struggle for life by the bare and square brick and slated workman's dwelling-house.

Happy the farm-labourer, if only he knew his own good-fortune, the painter murmured half unconsciously to himself (after the second Georgic), whose luck it was to dwell within those pretty, rose-clad, insanitary windows.

As he held his handsome head appreciatively on one side, and surveyed his own work with the complacent smile of the satisfied artist, an unexpected voice from behind startled him suddenly.

'What, Linnell!' the voice cried. 'You here, my dear fellow! I'd no idea of this. How lucky I met you!'

Linnell turned, blushing crimson like a girl. To say the truth, he hated to be caught in the obvious act of admiring his own poor tentative water-colours. 'Ha, ha, the prowling art-critic!' he answered, with a guilty air. 'Our avenging angel! We can never escape him. He dogs the trade like its own evil conscience. I didn't know, Mansel, you were looking over my shoulder and appraising my poor ineffective efforts.'

'Well, that's a nice way to welcome an old friend, after I don't know how many years that we haven't seen one another!' Mansel responded good-humouredly, grasping his hand hard with a friendly pressure. 'I steal upon you unawares from the middle distance, making sure it's you, in the full expectation of a warm reception; and I get called in return an avenging angel, and likened unwarrantably, out of pure wantonness, to the most hateful and baneful of created things, the crawling art-critic. For I, too, you know, have felt the creature bite my heel. I, too, have crushed the loathly worm. I, too, have suspended myself from a hook in Suffolk Street.'

Linnell wrung his old friend's hands warmly.

'You took me so by surprise,' he replied in

an apologetic tone. 'I'm afraid you must have thought me an awful fool, surveying my own handiwork with a complacent smirk, as if I were a Cox, or a Crome, or a Turner. But the fact is, my dear boy, every fellow on earth who paints at all must throw his whole heart into it; he must cultivate egotism, and believe in himself, or he'll never get other people to believe in him. Not that *I* believe in myself, for one moment, at bottom: I know I'm not worth a crooked sixpence, viewed as a painter. But don't think I didn't know you for a fellow-journeyman. I've seen your name at the Institute often, and admired your work too, if you'll allow me to say so. It's queer, indeed, we've never knocked up against one another accidentally anywhere since we left Christ Church.'

'Well, not so queer,' the other replied, 'if you take into consideration the patent fact that you go and bury yourself for half the year in the wilds of Africa, and only come to England for the other half, when all the rest of us are hard at work in Cornwall, or the Highlands, or Norway, or Switzerland. Very few artists frequent the desert in mid-December, and you never show up in winter in London.'

Linnell blushed again, this time with a faint flush of visible pleasure.

'You knew, then, that I spent the best part of my time in Egypt or Algiers?' he murmured timidly.

'My dear fellow, how could I call myself alive, I should like to know, if I hadn't admired those Moorish maidens with the wistful dark eyes and the Mohammedan voluptuousness, or those dim streets where veiled beauties mysteriously descend interminable steps of the native quarter, which testify to your existence in the Grosvenor annually? Not to know them would argue myself unknown with a vengeance. Everybody worth naming has seen and praised your glossy Nubians and your dreamy Arab girls.'

'No; have they, though, really?' Linnell echoed back with eager delight. 'I didn't know anyone (except the critics, confound them!) ever took the trouble to notice my things. There's so much good work in the Grosvenor always, that one naturally expects the *lesser* men to be passed by unheeded.'

'Besides,' Mansel continued, without rising to the fly, 'I've heard of you now and again from our neighbours, the Maitlands, who keep a villa or something of the sort over yonder at Algiers, and made your acquaintance there, you remember, last winter.'

Linnell's too expressive face fell slightly. If the secret must out, he preferred to be tracked by his handicraft alone.

'Why, yes,' he answered in a disappointed tone; 'of course I know the Maitlands well.

It's through them, to tell you the truth, that I'm here this summer. The old General knocked up against me in town last week, and asked me to run down and stop with them at High Ash. But I wouldn't accept the invitation outright, of course: I hate visiting—cramps individuality: I always like to be my own master. Besides, they've got a girl in the house, you see, and I bar girls, especially that one. She's a great deal too much up in the clouds for me, and she makes me fidgety. I prefer women who keep their feet planted on the solid ground. I was born on the earth, and I like to stop there. However, the old man's account of the place pleased me, and I've come down to stop at the Red Lion, accordingly, and do some sketching—or at least what I take, myself, for sketching—among the cliffs and cottages. From what you say, then, I infer you abide here.'

'You infer like a treatise on deductive logic.

We do abide here. We've got a bit of a *pied-à-terre* in a humble way on the hilltop yonder. A poor thing, but mine own. You must come and lunch with us this very morning.'

'Thanks. It's awfully good of you to think of bidding me. But you're married, I see. Inference again: you said *we*. Perhaps Mrs. Mansel won't be equally glad to see a perfect stranger at a moment's notice. Ladies object to the uninvited guest, not unreasonably. I'm not an old Oxford friend of *hers*, too, you know, my dear fellow.'

Mansel laughed.

'Oh, Ida won't mind, I'm sure,' he answered hastily, though with the internal qualms of the well-trained husband. 'She's quite accustomed to my Bohemian habits. I insist upon going out into the highways and byways and bringing home whomever I light upon. That's a pretty sketch of yours. As smooth as usual. Your quality's so good! and so much depth and breadth in the shadows of the doorway!'

Linnell put his head on one side once more, with a dubious air.

'Do you really think so?' he said, evidently reassured. 'Well, that's a comfort. I'm so glad you like it I was afraid, myself, the grays and yellows in the thatch were all wrong. They've bothered me terribly. Would you put a touch or so more of olive green for local colour in the dark corner by the deep-red creeper there? I'm not quite sure I've brought out the complementary shades under the eaves distinct enough.'

'Not another stroke!' Mansel answered decisively, eyeing it hard with his arms crossed. 'Not a dash! not a tinge! not a jot! not a thought even! You'd spoil the whole picture if you altered a single bit of the colouring there, I assure you. That's the fault of your detail, I've always said, if you won't be offended at an old friend's criticism. You spoil your best work by over-elaboration. I can see at a glance in all your most careful pieces—oh yes, I've studied them in Bond Street, you may be sure'—for Linnell had waved his hand deprecatingly—'that you do a good thing, and you do it to a turn, and then you're afraid to leave well alone; so you touch it up, and you touch it up, and you touch it up again, till all the breadth and force is taken clean out of it, and only the detail and the after-thoughts are left on your canvas.'

Linnell shook his head with a despondent air.

'It's too true,' he said slowly. 'I know it only too well myself already.'

'Well, then,' his friend answered with the prompt brusqueness of sound common-sense, 'be warned by experience, and avoid it in future. Don't go and do what you know's an error. Have the courage of your convictions, and leave off in time. The minute I looked at this bit on the easel, I said to myself: "By George! I didn't know Linnell had it in him." The ease and verve of the thing was just what I liked about it. And then, at the very moment when I'm standing admiring it, you propose to go and spoil the entire effect by faking it up to get the local colour strictly according to Cocker. Local colour and all the rules be hanged! The picture's the thing; and the picture's a vast deal better without them. Besides, I want you to get this particular sketch good. You know, of course, whose cottage you're painting?'

'No; I don't,' Linnell answered, surveying it carelessly. 'John Noakes's or Simon Stokes's, I should say, most probably.'

'Wrong!' Mansel cried, lowering his voice a trifle to a mysterious under-tone, for dim figures were flitting half unseen behind the high box hedge opposite. 'That poetical-looking cottage'—his tone sinking to a whisper—'you'll hardly believe it, but it's Haviland Dumaresq's.'

At that famous name, Linnell drew himself up in sudden surprise. If Mansel had counted upon producing an impression, he hadn't gone far wrong in his calculation. Linnell whistled a long low whistle.

'No; you're trying to take me in,' he exclaimed at last, after a short pause. 'We always called you "The Wag" at Christ Church, I remember. You can't surely mean Haviland Dumaresq the philosopher?'

Mansel smiled a smile of conscious superiority.

'You remind me of what Lewis Carroll said one evening at High Table,' he answered quickly, 'when we were all discussing the authorship of the Homeric poems. Everybody else had given his pet opinion on that endless problem, and while they all gabbled about it, Carroll sat and looked on grimly. At last somebody appealed to him for confirmation of his own special dogma. "Well," said Carroll, looking up in his dry way, "I've got a theory of my own about the 'Iliad' and 'Odyssey.' It is, that they weren't really written by Homer, but by another person of the same name." In Haviland Dumaresq's case, however, there's no room for any such doubt. No two people in the world could possibly be called by accident by such a singular combination of names as that. Don't shake your head. I'm quite in earnest. This is the original and only genuine Dumaresquian Theory. When you ask for the real Encyclopædic Philosophy, see that you get it. And here's the shop all the true stuff comes from.'

Linnell glanced up at his old college friend in breathless astonishment. For a moment it was clear he could hardly believe his own ears.

'Are you really serious?' he asked at last, gasping. 'I've always believed in Dumaresq most profoundly; and *I* can't suppose he inhabits a hovel. 'The Encyclopædic Philosophy' has almost put a girdle round the world in my own portmanteau. I never went anywhere that I didn't take it. And do you mean to tell me the man who wrote it—the philosopher who transcends space and time—the profoundest thinker of our age and nation—the greatest mathematician and deepest metaphysician in all Europe—really lives in a labourer's cottage?'

'Why not? Mansel answered with a screwed-up face. 'It's a very picturesque one.'

'Picturesque! *Je vous l'accorde.* But convenient, commodious, suitable, no. And painters as we are, we must still admit a man can't live on pure picturesqueness. Dirt and discomfort, I've always maintained, are necessary elements of the picturesque. But dirt and discomfort are personally distasteful in their actual form. It is only when painted that they become agreeable. What on earth can make a man like Haviland Dumaresq bury himself here, in such a mere cramped outhouse?'

'Poverty,' the local artist replied laconically.

'Poverty!' his friend echoed, all incredulous, a frank indignation flashing from his eye. 'You don't mean to tell me the man who first formulated that marvellous Law of Sidereal Reciprocity is still so poor that he has to inhabit a ploughman's hut in a remote village? For the honour of our kind, I refuse to believe it. I won't believe it; I can't believe it. It's a disgrace to the age. I knew Dumaresq was comparatively little read or known, of course—

that's the natural penalty of extreme greatness—but I always pictured the philosopher to myself as a wealthy man, living in easy circumstances in a London square, writing his books in a luxurious library, and serenely waiting for future generations to discover the true proportions of his stature. Bacon left his fame by will, you remember, to the care of foreign nations and the after-age. Foreign nations have found out Dumaresq already: the after-age will find him out in time, as surely as it found out Descartes and Newton.'

'You speak enthusiastically,' Mansel answered with a careless wave of his hand towards the rose-bound casements of the poetical cottage. 'I'm glad of that, for I'm always pleased when anybody comes here who has so much as heard poor old Dumaresq's name. The old man has led a life of continued neglect: that's the long and the short of it. All his hopes have been blighted and disappointed. His great work, though it's had here and there in all parts of the world a few glowing and fervid disciples like yourself, has fallen flat, for the most part, so far as public appreciation's concerned; and everything he expected to do he's failed in effecting. He seems to me always like a massive broken Egyptian pillar, rising among the ruins of Karnak or Luxor, as I see them rise in some of your own pictures.' Linnell's eye flashed with pleasure. 'And it's a great point for him to meet nowadays with anybody who sympathizes at all with his aims and his methods. He's had so little recognition in life, in fact, that, old as he is, a word of encouragement, a single compliment, an allusion to his work in ordinary conversation, seems to thrill him through and through with surprised enjoyment. I've seen him as pleased as a child at praise. He acknowledges it with a singular stately courtesy, as a right deferred, and holds his head higher in visible pride for the rest of that evening.'

'How pathetic!' Linnell cried. 'Yet I can easily believe it. What I can't believe is that Haviland Dumaresq should still be living in absolute poverty. I hope, when you say that, you don't mean me to take your words in the literal acceptation that he wants for money?'

'But I do, though, my dear fellow. I do—every word of it. The man's as poor as the proverbial church mouse. He never made a farthing out of the 'Encyclopædic Philosophy': it was dead loss from beginning to end: and he lives to this day from hand to mouth by doing the merest scientific hackwork for London publishers—Universal Instructors, you know, and that sort of clap-trap.'

With a sudden start, Linnell folded up his easel very resolutely. 'Come away,' he said in a firm voice. 'I can't stand this sort of thing, for my part, any longer. Haviland Dumaresq in want of money! Haviland Dumaresq lacking the bare means of support! Haviland Dumaresq buried in a pigsty! The thing's disgraceful. It's not to be endured! Why doesn't some rich person somewhere take the matter up and establish and endow him?'

'Some wealthy countryman of yours across the Atlantic, for example?' Mansel echoed good-humouredly. 'Well, yes, Americans are always fond of that earthly-providence business. I wonder, indeed, they've never thought of it.'

Linnell's face clouded visibly to the naked eye. 'What!' he cried, with unmistakable annoyance in his testy tone. 'That old mistake alive and green still! How often shall I have to correct the blunder! Didn't I tell you at Christ Church, over and over again, that I wasn't an American, and never had been—that I'd never a drop of Yankee blood in my veins—that my connection with Boston was a purely accidental one? My father merely settled there for—ur—for business purposes. We are not, and we never were, American citizens. I hate to be called what I'm not, and never will be. But that's neither here nor there at present. The question for the moment is simply this: Why doesn't somebody establish and endow Haviland Dumaresq?'

Mansel's face brimmed over with suppressed amusement.

'Establish and endow him!' he cried with a short laugh. 'My dear fellow, I'd like to see the man, American or otherwise, brave enough to suggest it to him for half a second. He'd better have a fast-trotting horse and a convenient gig waiting round the corner before he tries; for Haviland Dumaresq would forthwith arise and slay him with his hands, as King Arthur proposed to do to the good Sir Bedivere, unless he evacuated the premises with all reasonable haste before the old man could get up and at him. He's the proudest soul that ever stepped this earth, is Haviland Dumaresq. He'd rather starve than owe aught to any man. I can fancy how he'd take the proposal to subsidize him. The bare mention of the thing would kill him with humiliation.'

By this time Linnell had finished folding up his easel and picture, and addressed himself vigorously on the road homeward.

'What are you going for?' Mansel asked, with an innocent face.

'Going for?' Linnell repeated, with profound energy. 'Why, *something* must be done, I suppose, at once, about Dumaresq. This state of things is simply intolerable. A man with a world-wide reputation for the deepest thought among all who can think— that is to say, among all except absolute dolts and idiots—there, there, I haven't even patience to talk about it. *Something* must be done, I tell you, this very day, to set things square for him.'

'Exactly,' Mansel went on, gazing up at the sky in a vacant, far-away fashion. 'You're rich, we all know, Linnell, like the mines of Golconda. You drop as a universal provider from the clouds——'

He broke off suddenly, for Linnell had halted, and looked back at him half angrily, with a sudden quick suspicious glance.

'*I* rich!' the handsome young artist cried, with an impatient snap of his long middle finger. 'Again one of those silly old exploded Christ Church fallacies. Who ever told you I was rich, I'd like to know? You never had it from *my* lips, at any rate, Mansel. I wish unauthorized people wouldn't make one against one's will into a peg to hang startling myths and romances upon. A painter by trade, whose pictures only sell by accident, can never be rich—unless he has private means of his own, of course; works a gold mine or a Pennsylvanian oil-well. I own neither. Still, for all that, I feel it a burning shame to the times we live in that Haviland Dumaresq—the deepest thinker of our age and race—should end his days in a ploughman's cottage.'

CHAPTER II.

LINNELL'S MYSTERIES.

THEY turned aside into the deep-cut lane that led by tortuous twists toward the main road, and walked along for a second or two in solemn silence. Mansel was the first to break their reverie.

'Why, Linnell,' he cried, with a start of astonishment, pointing down to his friend's feet with an awkward gesture, 'you're all right again that way now, then, are you? You—you don't find your leg trouble you any longer?'

Till that moment, the new-comer to Petherton had been strolling along easily and naturally enough; but almost as the words passed Mansel's lips, the older resident noticed that Linnell was now limping a little with his left foot—an imperceptible limp to a casual observer, though far more marked within the last few seconds than it had been a minute or two before attention was called to it. Linnell glanced down and smiled uneasily.

'Oh, I hobble along rather better than I used to do,' he answered casually, with an evasive laugh. 'They sent me to Egypt for that, you know. Dry as blazes in Egypt. The old affection was rheumatic in origin, it seems. Damp intensified it. I was told a warm climate might do me good. Sir Anthony Wraxall — astute old beggar— advised me never to let myself feel cold in my limbs for a single moment; and I've done my best ever since to follow out his directions to the letter. I've spent every winter for the last five years on the Nile or in Algeria. I've camped out for weeks together in the middle of the desert; I've dressed half my time like an Arab chief to give my limbs free play: I've ridden all day long on my horse or my camel: I've never walked when I could possibly get a mount of any sort: and in the end, I'm beginning to hobble about, I'm glad to say, in a way that remotely resembles walking. I suppose the treatment's getting me round at last a bit.'

'Resembles walking,' Mansel exclaimed, with surprise. 'Why, my dear fellow, you can walk every bit as well as all the rest of us. To tell you the truth, you stood so firm, and turned about and walked off so naturally, that I'd almost forgotten, at the first blush, all about your old difficulty.'

'That was because I was excited and indignant about poor old Dumaresq,' Linnell answered hastily, with obvious embarrassment. 'I always walk better when I'm emotionally roused. It takes my mind off. I forget I've legs. When I play lawn-tennis, I never think for the time being about my lameness. It's when my attention's called to the existence of my feet that I feel it worst. Self-consciousness, I suppose. But don't let's discuss me. The empirical ego's always tedious. There are so many other much more interesting subjects than an individual man to talk about in the universe!'

'I'm not so sure of that,' Mansel replied reflectively. 'Man, says Emerson, is perennially interesting to man; and I always like to hear about you, Linnell. I expect another winter or two 'll set you up completely. Why, my dear fellow, where are you going off to? You're coming to lunch with us, aren't you? That's our little box, you see— up there on the hill-top.'

'Oh, thank you,' Linnell answered, gazing round him abstractedly. 'But I don't think I'll come in to lunch to-day, if you please. I've too much respect for Mrs. Mansel's feelings. If you'll allow me, I'll drop in upon you this afternoon, and pay my respects first in due form—and respectable clothes— to your wife and family. In England, you know, all things must be done decently and in order.'

'But not in Bohemia, my dear fellow: not in Bohemia.'

Linnell glanced down nervously upon the deep-blue bay.

'Your Bohemia and Shakespeare's are much the same, it seems,' he answered, smiling. 'Each is provided with a sea-coast, gratis, by poetical license. But I won't avail myself of your kindness, for all that. I'll go back to the inn first and change my suit. These shabby old painting-things aren't fit company for ladies' society. This afternoon, if you'll allow me to call, I shall hope to come up, arrayed like Solomon in all his glory, and leave my card respectfully upon Mrs. Mansel.'

A sudden thought seemed to strike the would-be host.

'You're a bachelor, of course?' he exclaimed interrogatively.

Linnell's eye wandered down once more, with a timid glance, towards his left foot.

'Do you suppose a painter whose works don't sell would be likely to burden any woman on earth with *that*?' he asked, somewhat bitterly—'least of all, a woman whom he loved and respected?'

'Come, come, Linnell!' the other man cried, with genuine kindliness. 'This is too ridiculous: quite overwrought, you know. You carry your sensitiveness a deal too far. A fine, manly, handsome fellow like you—

an upstanding man, who can ride, and swim, and play lawn-tennis—to talk like that—why, it's simple nonsense. I should think any girl in her senses would be glad enough, if she could, to catch you.'

'That's the way you married men always talk,' Linnell answered shortly. 'As soon as you've secured a wife for yourselves, you seem to lose all the chivalry in your nature. You speak as if every woman were ready to jump at the very first man who happens to ask her. That may be the way, I dare say, with a great many of them. If so, they're not the sort I'd care to marry. There are women *and* women, I suppose, as there are fagots *and* fagots. I prefer, myself, the shrinking variety—the kind that accepts a man for his own sake, not for the sake of getting married merely.'

'You know what the Scotch girl said when her parents represented to her the various faults of the scapegrace who'd proposed to her?' Mansel put in, laughing. '" Oo, ay," she said; "but he's aye a man, ye ken." And you have there in a nutshell the whole philosophy of the entire matter. Still, setting aside all that, even, I know no man more likely——'

Linnell brushed him aside with his hand hastily.

'Well, here our roads part,' he said, with some decision in his tone, like one who wishes to check an unpleasant argument. 'I'll see you again this afternoon, when I've made my outer man fit for polite society. Till then, good-bye;' and with a swinging pace he walked off quickly down the steep hill, erect and tall, his easel and picture slung carelessly by his side, and no trace of lameness perceptible anywhere in his rapid stride and manly carriage.

Mansel gazed after him with a painter's

admiration for a well-built figure. 'As good-looking a fellow as ever stepped,' he thought to himself in silent criticism. 'What a pity he insists on torturing himself all his life long with these meaningless apprehensions and insoluble mysteries!'

He strolled up slowly to his own gate. In the garden, his wife was busy with the geraniums—a pretty young girl, in a light summer dress and a big straw hat that suited her admirably. 'Ida,' he cried out, as he swung open the wicket, 'who do you think is stopping at the Lion? I met him just now, in Middle Mill Fields, doing a water-colour of Dumaresq's cottage. Why, Linnell of Christ Church. You recollect, I've often told you all about him.'

'What, the lame man, Reggy, who had the dog that ran after the Proctor?'

'Well, he used to be lame once, but he isn't now a bit—at least, not to speak of:

you'd hardly notice it. Still, though the lameness itself's gone, it seems to have left him just as sensitive and nervous as ever—or a great deal more so. He's coming up here this afternoon to call on you, though, and you'll be able to judge of him then for yourself: but as far as I can see, there's nothing on earth left for the man to be sensitive about. Make much of him, Ida: he's as timid as a girl; but he's a nice fellow for all that, in spite of his little mysteries and mystifications.'

'He's a painter, too, isn't he?' Mrs. Mansel sked, arranging a flower in her husband's button-hole. 'I think you showed me some things of his once at the Grosvenor or the Academy.'

'Yes; he daubs like the rest of us—does the Nubian Girl trick and the Street in Cairo dodge; not badly either. But he's taken all that up since I last saw him. He was the merest amateur in black and white when we were at Oxford together. Now he paints like a man who's learnt his trade, though he rather overdoes things in the matter of elaboration. Works at textures till you can't see the picture for the painting. But I don't believe he can live on his art, for all that. He's rich, I imagine, though for some strange reason he won't allow it. But that's his way. He's full of all sorts of little fads and fancies. He makes it a rule never to admit anything, except by torture. He's an American born, and he calls himself an Englishman. He spends money right and left, and he calls himself a pauper. He's straight and good-looking, and he calls himself a cripple. His name Linnell, and he calls himself Linnéll. In fact, he's all made up of endless little ideas and affectations.'

'There's a Sir Austen Linnéll down our way in Rutland,' his wife said musingly as they turned towards the house, 'and *he* calls himself Linnéll too, with the accent the same way on the second syllable. Perhaps your friend and the Rutland man may be some sort of relations.'

'Can't, my dear child. Don't I tell you he's American? No baronets there: Republican simplicity. Boston born, though he hates to be told so. The star-spangled banner's a red rag to him. Avoid chaffing him, for heaven's sake, about the hub of the universe.'

They had entered the drawing-room while they spoke by the open French windows, and Mrs. Mansel, in a careless way, took up from the table by the corner sofa a Grosvenor catalogue. 'Ah, this must be he,' she said, turning over the leaves to the alphabetical list: 'See here—"329, The Gem of the Harem; 342, By the Edge of the Desert: Charles Austen Linnell." Why, Reggy, just look: his name's Austen; and he spells it with an *e* too, exactly like the Rutland people. I don't care whatever *you* choose to say— American or no American, he and the Austen Linnells of Thorpe *must* be related to one another.'

Her husband took the little book from her hands incredulously. 'Not possible,' he murmured, gazing hard at the page. 'I'm not quite sure, but I fancy I've heard it said at Christ Church there was something wrong somewhere about the family pedigree. Linnell's father made his money out of a quack medicine or something of the sort over in America, and sent his son to Oxford, accordingly, to make a gentleman of him, and get rid of the rhubarb and sarsaparilla. They say Linnell would never go back to his native land again after he took his degree, because he hated to see all the rocks on the Hudson River and all the peaks of the White Mountains plastered over in big white letters with the touching inscription, "Use only Linnell's Instantaneous Lion Liver Pills." At least, so Gregory of Brasenose told me, and his father, I fancy, was once an *attaché* or *chargé d'affaires* at Washington.'

'But how does he come to be called Austen, then?' Mrs. Mansel went on with true feminine persistency, sticking to her point like a born woman. 'And Austen with an *e* too! That clinches the argument. If it was only an *i*, now, it might perhaps be accidental: but don't go telling me Austen with an *e* comes within the limits of anything less than a miraculous coincidence.'

Her husband glanced over her shoulder once more at the catalogue she had seized and examined a second time. 'It's odd,' he said after a pause—'distinctly odd. I see the finger of design in this, undoubtedly. It can't be accident, as you justly remark with your usual acumen: mere coincidence, as you observe, always stops short at phonetic spelling. And now you mention it, I remember Sir Austen does not spell his name with an *e* certainly: I had a cheque from him once for " The Smugglers' Refuge "—that picture we let go too cheap, Ida. But there are two ways of accounting for it, all the same: there are always at least two good ways of accounting for everything—except the action of a hanging committee. Either Linnell's descended from a younger branch of the Rutland family, which went out to America in the *Mayflower*—all good Boston people, I understand, made it a point of honour to go out in the *Mayflower*, which must have had accommodation for at least as many first-class cabin passengers as the whole fleet that came over with William the Conqueror—or else, failing that, his excellent papa must with rare forethought have christened him Austen in order to produce a delusive impression on the public mind in future years that he belonged to a distinguished and aristocratic county family. Godfathers and godmothers at one's baptism do often perpetrate these pious frauds. I knew a man once whose real surname was plain Dish; but his parents with great presence of mind christened him Spencer Caven, so he grew up to be Spencer Cavendish, and everybody thought he was a second cousin of the Duke of Devonshire.'

Mrs. Mansel, for her part, had been educated at Girton. So superficial a mode of settling a question by pure guesswork offended her views of logical completeness.

'It's no use arguing *a priori*, Reginald,' she said seriously, 'upon a matter of experience. We can ask Mr. Linnell about it when he comes here this afternoon. I've invited Mr. Dumaresq and Psyche to drop in for a set of tennis, and your Christ Church friend 'll be just in time for it.'

When Mrs. Mansel got upon *a priori* and *a posteriori*, her husband, who was only a painter, after all, knew his place too well to answer her back in the same dialect. He only stared at the catalogue harder than ever, and wondered to himself in a vague way why Linnell should call himself Austen.

But at that very moment, at the Red Lion, the artist himself was sitting down at the little davenport to dash off a hasty and excited note to his agent in London :

'DEAR MATTHEWS,

'Can you get some fellow who knows all about such things to give you an exhaustive list of all the public libraries or institutions in Great Britain, Ireland, America, or the colonies, to which a man interested in the matter might present a complete set of Haviland Dumaresq's "Encyclopædic Philosophy"? The bigger the number you can hunt up the better. Perhaps the people at the London Institution would put you in the way of finding it out. In any case, try to draw up a good big catalogue, and forward it here to me at your earliest convenience. But on no account let anyone know why you want the information. I've sent a cheque for fifty guineas to that poor fellow you wrote about at Colchester: many thanks for calling my attention to his painful case. Only I could have wished he wasn't a German. Teutonic distress touches me less nearly. Never mind about buying-in those New Zealands at present. I see another use for the money I meant to put in them. In breathless haste to save post,

'Yours ever sincerely,
'CHARLES AUSTEN LINNELL.'

'There,' he said to himself as he folded it up and consigned it to its envelope: 'that'll do a little good, I hope, for Dumaresq. The only possible use of money to a fellow like me, whose tastes are simple, and whose wants are few, is to shuffle it off as well as he can upon others who stand in greater need of it. The worst of it is, one spends one's life in that matter, perpetually steering between the Scylla of pride and the Charybdis of pauperism. The fellows who really need help won't take it, and the fellows who don't need it are always grabbing at it. There's a deal too much reserve and sensitiveness in the world—and I've got my own share too, as well as the rest of them.'

CHAPTER III.

LOVE—THIRTY.

WHEN Linnell appeared upon the Mansels' tennis-ground at half-past three that afternoon, it was in quite other garb from the careless painter suit he had worn on the hillside in the incognito of morning. He was arrayed now in the correctest of correct gray tweeds, and the most respectable of round felt hats, in place of the brown velveteens and Rembrandt cap wherewith he had sallied forth, to the joy of all young Petherton, at early morn for his day's sketching. Yet it was difficult to say in which of the two costumes he looked handsomest—the picturesque artistic suit of the cosmopolitan painter, or the simple rough homespun country dress of the English gentleman Linnell was tall, and very dark: his deep black eyes were large and expressive; and his rough beard and moustache, trimmed with a certain loose touch of artistic freedom, gave a decided tone of manliness and vigour to what might otherwise have seemed too purely cultivated and refined a face. As it was, nobody could look at Charles Linnell without seeing in him at a glance the best product of our English school and college training—a man first, and afterwards a gentleman.

As he crossed the lawn to where Mrs. Mansel sat on a rustic chair under the shade of the big umbrella-like lime-tree, he saw that two other visitors were already before him, each of whom equally attracted at once the artist's quick and appreciative eye. The first was indeed a noble presence—a tall and thin old man, gray-haired and gray-moustached, clad in a close-fitting light pea-jacket and slouch hat, which seemed to bring out in singular relief the full height and spareness of his long lithe figure. No one could have passed that figure by unnoticed even in the crowded streets of London. The old man's face was full of vividness, fire, and innate majesty. Though close on seventy, he was young still in expression and bearing: he held his gray head proudly erect, and the light that flashed from his keen and deep-set eyes was instinct even now with youthful vigour and unquenchable energy. The high arched forehead, the projecting eyebrows, the sharp clear features, the strong and masculine chin, the delicate mouth, instinct with irony, the powerful lines scored deep on the thin cheeks and round the speaking corners of the acute gray eyes, all told alike of profound intellectual strength and subtlety. The very movements of his limbs were free and unrestrained: he stood aside two steps for Linnell to approach with something of the statuesque Greek gracefulness. The artist had no need to wait for an introduction. He felt sure instinctively it was Haviland Dumaresq, the Encyclopædic Philosopher, who stood in the flesh there visibly before him.

The other stranger, no less striking in her way, was a young girl of sixteen or seventeen, in the first flush of a delicate pink-and-white, peach-like beauty. Linnell was so taken by her childish face and graceful form that he had hardly time to bestow a passing glance upon the maturer and more matronly attractiveness of their common hostess. Even so, he was but dimly aware of a pair of soft and full round cheeks, mantled by a dainty suffused bloom, and with a temptingly rosy mouth set full beneath them, too simple as yet to be even coquettish. Linnell was a shy man, and Haviland Dumaresq's presence at once overawed him. He was so much agitated by the stately courtesy—a courtesy as of the grand old courtly school—with which the great thinker had stridden aside two paces to let him pass, that he could fix his eyes steadily neither on Mrs. Mansel nor on her pretty little visitor. The lawn swam in a vague haze of uncertainty around him, out of all which only the tall spare figure on the one hand, and that pair of rose-petal cheeks on the other, loomed distinctly visible through the mist of his own shyness on his perturbed and unsteady mental vision.

Happily Mansel came forward to his aid in the nick of time.

'Ida,' he said to his wife as she rose from her seat to meet and greet the new-comer, 'this is my friend Linnell of whom you've heard me speak often. Linnell, let me introduce you to Mr. Dumaresq, whose work you know and appreciate so deeply already. Psyche, this is a dear old Oxford friend of mine: he paints pictures, so you're sure to like him.'

Linnell bowed all round at each introduction with mechanical politeness. So many new acquaintances all at once, one of them distinguished, and two pretty, were far too much for his unstable composure. He muttered some inarticulate conventional phrase, and looked about him uncomfortably at the lawn and the garden.

Haviland Dumaresq himself was the first to break the awkward silence.

'Linnell,' he repeated in a rich and powerful but very silvery voice: 'I hope I caught the name correctly—Linnell. Ah, yes; I thought so. One seldom catches a name right at a first introduction, because all hearing is largely inference; and here, where no context exists to guide one's guesses, inference is impossible. The world is all before one where to choose: any one name is just as likely to occur in an introduction as another. You said Linnéll, with the accent on the last, I notice, Mansel. I'm a student of names—among other things'—and he looked the artist keenly in the face with a searching glance. 'I've only met the name, so accented, once before. Sir Austen Linnell was with me at Trinity—not the present man, of course—his father, the General. They're all Sir Austen Linnells in succession in the Rutland family—have been ever since the Restoration, in fact, when the first man was created a Baronet for welcoming King Charles the moment he landed.'

'Mr. Linnell's name's Austen, too,' Mrs. Mansel put in suavely, as she reseated herself with Girtonian grace on the rustic chair. 'We happened to look you up in the Grosvenor Catalogue this morning, Mr. Linnell—

I couldn't recollect the name of that sweet picture of yours, " The Gem of the Harem ": Reggy and I admired it immensely this year on varnishing day. And there we found you set down at full length as Charles Austen Linnell, you know ; and we wondered whether you mustn't be related to the Rutland people.'

'Austen with an *e*,' Haviland Dumaresq interposed with great gravity. 'Names of similar sound but different in spelling are almost always of distinct origin. Phonetic decay assimilates primarily unlike words. Tur*ner*, for example, is only plain turner, a man who puts wood in a lathe for chairs and tables; but Tur*nor* with an *o*, like the Turnors of Norfolk, are really Tour Noirs, of Norman origin. There the assimilation is obviously late and obviously phonetic.' For it was a peculiarity of Haviland Dumaresq's mind, as Linnell soon learned, that he saw nothing—not even the merest small-talk—as isolated fact: every detail came to him always as a peg on which to hang some abstract generalization. The man was pure philosopher to the core: he lived in the act of organizing events by squads and battalions into orderly sequence. To Linnell himself, however, the timely diversion came very pleasantly: he hated his own personality, or his own name even, to form the subject of public discussion.

But he wasn't permitted to rejoice over the side-issue long. Mrs. Mansel brought the conversation back again at a bound, with feminine instinct, to the purely personal and immediate question.

'Mr. Linnell spells *his* Austen with an *e*, too,' she said briskly. 'I suppose, Mr. Linnell, you're a member of the same old Rutland family?'

Haviland Dumaresq turned round upon him once more with a strange display of earnest interest. Linnell hesitated. His face was crimson.

'Of the same family,' he repeated after a pause, with obvious reluctance; then he added with a little sidelong, suspicious look: 'but the younger son of a younger son only. I hardly even know my cousin, Sir Austen, the head of the house. Junior branches are seldom held of much account, of course, in an English family.'

'Primogeniture is a great injustice to the elder sons,' Haviland Dumaresq murmured reflectively in his measured tones. 'It deprives them of all proper stimulus to action. It condemns them to a life of partridge-shooting and dinner-giving. It stunts and dwarfs their mental faculties. It robs them of all that makes life worth living. Still, it has its compensating advantages as well, in the long-run, for the nation at large. By concentrating the whole fortune of able and successful families—judges, bishops, new peers, and so forth, the cream of their kind, who have risen by their own ability to the top, leaving the mere skim-milk of humanity at the bottom—on one single rich and useless representative, the scapegoat, as it were, of the family opulence, it turns the younger sons adrift upon the world, with their inherited intellect for their sole provision, and so urges them on to exceptional effort, in order to keep up their positions in society, and realize their natural expectations and the hopes of their upbringing. I'm not sure that it isn't a good thing, after all, for an aristocratic community that a certain number of its ablest members should be left to shift for themselves by their own wits, and, after having been brought up in comfort and luxury with a good education, should be forced at last to earn their own living in the hard struggle for life which is the rule of nature.'

'But all younger sons are not poor,' the girl they called Psyche put in blushingly.

Linnell turned to her with a quick, keen glance.

'Not quite all, perhaps,' he said with a decisive accent; 'but so large a proportion of the total sum, that you may almost take it for granted about any of them whenever you meet one.'

His interposition turned the current of the conversation. They sat for a few minutes talking trivialities about the beauty of the place and Linnell's first impressions of Petherton Episcopi; then Mansel said, turning to the philosopher:

'Where do you think I picked up my friend this morning, Mr. Dumaresq? He was at work on the slope yonder, sketching your cottage.'

'It's a pretty cottage,' Dumaresq answered with a slight inclination of his leonine head.

'So bright and fluffy. The prettiest place I've ever seen. I've always admired my own cottage.'

'Oh, papa,' Psyche broke in, red-faced, incidentally settling for Linnell, off-hand, the hitherto moot-question of her personal identity, 'it's so *very* tiny!'

'For you, my child, yes,' the father answered tenderly. 'But for me, no. It exactly fits me. My niche in nature is a very humble one. In all those matters I'm a perfect Stoic of the old school. I ask no more from fate or fortune than the chances of the Cosmos spontaneously bestow upon me.'

'It makes a very pretty sketch,' Linnell interposed gently, in his diffident way. 'Will you allow an old admirer of the "Encyclopædic Philosophy"—perhaps one of your earliest and most devoted adherents—to present it to you as a memento—a disciple's fee, so to speak— when finished?'

Dumaresq looked him back in the face with an undecided air. He drummed his fingers dubitatively on his knee for a minute. Then, 'You are a professional artist?' he asked slowly.

'A professional artist? Well, yes, of course; I sell my pictures—whenever I can; and as far as I'm able, I try to live upon them.'

'Then I must *buy* the sketch,' Dumaresq answered, with a quiet and stately decision in his manner. 'If you'd been an amateur, now, I would gladly have accepted it from you; but I, too, am a workman, and I have my principles. In art, as in literature, science, and thought, the labourer, we remember, is worthy of his hire. I should like to have a fitting presentment of our little home. It would be nice for Psyche to possess it hereafter.'

The calm dignity and precision of his tone

took Linnell fairly by surprise. The man couldn't have spoken with more majestic carelessness if he had been the lordly owner of five thousand acres, commissioning a Leighton or an Alma Tadema. Yet Linnell had only to look at his own studiously simple threadbare dress, and the neat quietness of his daughter's little print, to see that five pounds was a large matter to him. The picture when completed would be worth full fifty.

'We won't quarrel about that,' the artist said hastily, with a little deprecatory wave of his white hand. 'I'll show you the sketch as soon as it's finished, and then we may perhaps effect an equitable exchange for it. Or at least'—and he glanced shyly on one side towards Psyche—'I may possibly be permitted to offer it by-and-by for Miss Dumaresq's acceptance.'

The old man was just about to answer with a hurried refusal, when Mansel intervened with a pacificatory remark. 'Linnell was telling me this morning,' he said, dragging it in by all-fours, 'how greatly he admired and respected your philosophic system. He has all your doctrines at his fingers' ends; and he was quite surprised to find an ungrateful world didn't crowd to Petherton in its millions, by excursion train, to pay you the tribute of its respect and consideration. He means to have some royal confabs with you on Dumaresquian subjects whenever you can spare him an hour or two of your valuable leisure.'

'Papa sees so few people here who care at all for the questions he's interested in,' Psyche said, looking up, 'that he's always delighted and pleased when he really lights upon a philosophic visitor and gets a chance of exchanging serious opinions.'

The old man's face flushed like a child's with ingenuous pleasure; appreciation cam so late to him, and came so rarely, that it went to his heart with pathetic keenness; but he gave no sign of his emotion by spoken words. He merely answered, in the same sonorous silvery voice as before: 'Philosophy has necessarily a restricted audience. Intelligence being the special property of the few, the deeper and wider and more important a study, the narrower must needs be the circle of its possible students.'

Mrs. Mansel tapped her parasol impatiently. Girton-bred as she was, she yet believed by long experience it was possible to have too much of poor dear old Dumaresq.

'Psyche, my child,' she said, yawning under cover of her Japanese fan, 'shall we go on now and have our game of tennis?'

They fell into their places in the court as if by accident, Psyche and the new-come artist on one side, Mansel and his wife opposite them on the other. Dumaresq sat by observant, and watched the play; it always interested him to look on at tennis: the run of the balls is so admirably pregnant with suggestive ideas for sidereal motions!

As for Psyche, she never before had enjoyed a game with anyone so much. Linnell was so handsome, and played so admirably. In the excitement of the game, he had quite forgotten his lameness now, and remembered only the quick sight and nimble movement of his desert experiences. No man in England could play tennis better, indeed, when he managed to drop out of mind his infirmities; and that afternoon he was happily able to drop them altogether. He remembered only that Psyche was beautiful, and that to play with Haviland Dumaresq's daughter was something very different indeed from playing with the common nameless herd of squireen femininity on the lawn of the vicarage in some country village.

For to Linnell, Haviland Dumaresq's was so great a name as to throw some reflected halo even around Psyche.

As father and daughter walked home alone, after five o'clock tea, in the cool of the evening, to their tiny cottage—the old man tall, erect, and grim; Psyche one rosebud blush from chin to forehead—Haviland Dumaresq stopped for a second at the turn of the road, and gazing at his daughter with a lingering affection, said abruptly:

'I felt I must buy it. I was obliged to buy it. I couldn't take it from the man for nothing, of course. Whatever it costs, I shall have to pay for it.'

'How much is it worth, do you think, papa?' Psyche asked, half trembling.

'I know so little about this sort of thing,' the old philosopher answered gravely; 'but I shouldn't be in the least surprised to learn he wanted as much as ten pounds for it.'

'Ten pounds is an awful lot of money!' Psyche cried, affrighted.

'Ten pounds is a very large sum indeed,' her father echoed, repeating the phrase in his own dialect. 'Too large a sum for anyone to waste upon a piece of paper with the image or simulacrum of a common dwelling-house scrawled in colour upon it. But there was no help for it; I had to do it. Otherwise, the man might have pressed the thing upon me as a mere present. And a present's an obligation I never can accept. We can save the necessary amount, perhaps, by giving up all needless luxuries for breakfast, and taking only tea and bread without butter.'

'Oh, papa!' Psyche murmured, aghast.

'Not you, my child, not you!' the father answered hurriedly. 'I never meant you, my darling—but myself and Maria. I think the existing culinary utensil calls herself Maria.'

'But, my dear, dear father——'

'Not a word, my child. Don't try to interfere with me. I know what's best for us, and I do it unhesitatingly. I must go through the world on my own orbit. The slightest attempt to turn a planet from its regular course recoils destructively upon the head of the aggressive body that crosses its cycle. I'm a planetary orb, obeying fixed laws: I move in my circuit undeterred and unswerving.'

They walked along a few yards farther in silence. Then Haviland Dumaresq spoke again.

'He belongs to a very good family, that painting young man,' he said, with a jerk of his head towards the Mansels'. 'The Linnells of Rutland are distinguished people. But he's a younger son, and worth nothing. A younger son, and got no money. Lives on his pictures. Worth nothing.'

'Papa!' Psyche cried, in a ferment of astonishment, unable to suppress her surprise and wonder. 'What a funny thing for *you* to say—you, of all men, who care nothing at all for money or position. He's very clever, I think, and very handsome, and I know he's read the " Encyclopædic Philosophy." '

Dumaresq held his proud gray head prouder and higher still against the evening sky.

'I mean,' he said evasively, 'the young man's poor. An artist who hardly lives on his art. All the more reason, then (if it comes to that), to pay for his picture. His time's his money.'

But Psyche herself vaguely knew in her own heart that that was nothing more than an excuse and an afterthought. She knew what her father really meant. She knew and wondered. For never before in all her life had Psyche Dumaresq heard that austere philosopher reckon up any man by his fortune or his family. And why should he make so unfavourable an exception against so pleasant a person as this new young painter?

She didn't understand the simple and well-known human principle that no man is a philosopher when he has daughters to marry.

CHAPTER IV.

A PROPHET IS NOT WITHOUT HONOUR.

The next evening Linnell was to dine quietly at General Maitland's. Only a few Petherton friends to meet him—'quite a simple affair, you know, Mr. Linnell: the regulation country-town entertainment: our next-door neighbours: just to introduce you to whatever there is of society at Petherton Episcopi.' The Mansels were coming: of course the Mansels: and the Vicar and his wife, and the Craigies from the Manor House.

'But not, I suppose, that old bore Dumaresq, and that gawky girl of his?' the General observed, as they sat in the drawing-room, demurely expectant, on the very stroke of half-past seven. 'He talks me off my legs with his crack-jaw philosophy. You haven't asked *them*, I do hope, Maria.'

'Do you take me for a fool, George?' Mrs. Maitland answered with severe dignity, drawing herself up austerely to her full height. 'Geraldine begged me to ask them, I need hardly say: she has no common-sense at all, poor dear Geraldine: but I was firm upon that point, perfectly firm'—and Mrs. Maitland's high-bred chin and thin lips of the Vere de Vere caste showed her firmness most distinctly as she spoke. 'I put my foot down upon that sort of nonsense once for all. I said to her plainly: Geraldine, you may form what undesirable acquaintances you like for yourself; but you shall not drag your poor papa and me into the thick of your vulgar society. I've called upon that horrid old man and his daughter on your account, and I very much regret now that I ever did it. It lets us in for endless complications. The Dumaresqs are people who move in a different grade of society from our own, and any attempt to take them out of it and put them into one for which they're not fitted can only be painful, and even ignominious, to both parties. I said it plainly to her, "even ignominious." The fact is, George, we ought never to have known them. When one has to deal with a girl of poor dear Geraldine's unfortunate temperament, the only way to do is to resist at once from the very beginning all her absurd fads and fancies.'

The General sighed. 'It's a pity she won't be more practical,' he said with a faint reluctance in his voice, for he admired Geraldine. 'She's a fine girl, though she's our own daughter, Maria, and, by George! I like her for it. I like to see a girl stick up for her opinions. Still, it's a great pity, I don't deny, she won't be more practical. If only she'd take a fancy, now, to this young Linnell there!'

'This young Linnell has money,' Mrs. Maitland assented curtly, arranging a spray of maidenhair in a specimen glass on the table by the bow window. 'I'm sure he has money. He won't admit it; but it's perfectly clear to anybody with half an eye. He couldn't live as he does upon his pictures only.'

'And you think?' the General observed suggestively.

'I think he hasn't come down here for nothing, naturally,' Mrs. Maitland went on with marked emphasis. 'He was very much struck with Geraldine at Algiers, I feel sure; but his head's stuffed as full of flighty sentimental nonsense as her own: and if he's thrown in with that blushing bread-and-butter slip of a girl of poor old Dumaresq's, he'll fancy himself in love with her just because she's poor and pretty and a nobody. That kind of man always does go and throw himself away upon a nobody, unless he's closely watched, and protected by others against his own folly. Geraldine's built the very same way. Nothing on earth would give her greater delight, I'm sure, than to marry a penniless poet, or painter, or music-master, and end her days with him comfortably in the workhouse.'

The General toyed with the Japanese paper-knife uneasily. 'It's a great pity she can't get settled,' he said after a pause. 'With Hugh's expenses at Sandhurst so very heavy; and Gordon at Aldershot always asking for remittances, remittances, and again remittances, till one's sick and tired of it; and the two boys at the Charterhouse eating their heads off and doing nothing; it's really very much to be regretted, indeed, that she can't find anybody anywhere to suit her. And yet,

Maria, I sympathize a great deal, after all, with Geraldine. A girl naturally prefers to wait and watch till she's found the man that really suits her.'

'It's not as if she met no young men,' Mrs. Maitland went on, ignoring quietly her husband's last rebellious sentence, 'or never had any suitable offers. I'm sure no girl in England has been given better or greater chances. She was very much admired, indeed, at Aldershot: she goes to all the dances in Algiers: she's been up in town for three seasons running: she travels about fifty times more than most girls do: and that man in the 42nd with the scar on his cheek would certainly have married her if only she'd have taken him, stammer or no stammer. I never knew anyone more difficult to please or more impossible for an anxious mother to count upon.'

Their conversation was cut short abruptly

at that moment by the entry of the peccant Geraldine in person. She was tall and dark, with fine features, a little marred, perhaps, by a certain conscious pride and dignity ; but her strong chin was instinct with character, and her upright carriage spoke her at once a woman with a will not to be bent even by a conscientiously worldly mother like Mrs. Maitland. Her father looked up at her with a glance of sidelong, surreptitious approbation as she entered. 'Those passion-flowers become you, Geraldine,' he said, with a furtive side-look at his formidable wife. 'They're very pretty. Where did you get them?'

'Psyche gave them to me,' Geraldine answered with a careless touch or two of her fingers on the drooping spray that hung gracefully down from her shapely neck over the open bosom. 'They have a pale-blue passion-flower growing over their porch, you know, and Psyche picked me a few blossoms off it to

wear this evening. She's such a dear, always.
They *do* look well, I think. Unusual things
like that always suit me.'

'You went round there this afternoon,
then ?' her mother asked.

Geraldine nodded a quiet assent.

' Psyche asked me to come round,' she said.
' She's full of Mr. Linnell. She wanted to
know from me all about him.'

Mrs. Maitland glanced up sharply with
quick, inquiring eyes.

'Why, what on earth does she know of
him ?' she inquired half angrily. ' Has she
met him anywhere ?'

' She met him yesterday afternoon at the
Mansels',' Geraldine answered shortly.

' And what did you tell her, Geraldine ?
You didn't let her know he was rich, I
suppose, did you ?'

' How could I, mother ? He always implies
himself that he isn't. Even if I thought it,

which I've no reason to do, it would be very wrong of me to say so to Psyche. I told her he was a most agreeable young man, though painfully shy and awkward and nervous, and that we knew him only as an English painter who often wintered in Egypt or Algeria.'

Mrs. Maitland breathed more freely for a moment. Next instant there came a small ring at the bell, and the servant, entering, announced Mr. Linnell, followed in a minute more by both the Mansels.

Linnell took Geraldine in to dinner; but being the guest of the evening, he was sandwiched in between herself and her mother, an arrangement which ensured the possibility for Mrs. Maitland of exercising throughout an efficient supervision over Geraldine's conversation with the eligible stranger.

'And how do you like Petherton now you've fairly settled down to it?' Mrs. Maitland asked him as the soup went round. 'Have you found any subjects for sketching yet, Mr. Linnell?'

The young man looked up with an embarrassed smile. If there was anything on earth that his soul hated it was 'being trotted out,' on his art especially; and he saw quite clearly that Mrs. Maitland meant to trot him out in due course this evening, in order to exhibit his paces properly before the admiring eyes of Petherton society.

'Yes,' he answered shyly, with half an appealing glance towards Mrs. Mansel opposite; 'I began to sketch a sweet little cottage on the hillside yesterday; and when I'd got half-way through with it, I learnt, to my surprise, it was no less a personage's than Haviland Dumaresq's. I'd no idea, Mrs. Maitland, you had so great a man as the Encyclopædic Philosopher living in your neighbourhood.'

'Oh yes, Mr. Dumaresq's very clever, I believe,' Mrs. Maitland answered somewhat frigidly, with the austere manner which the British matron thinks it proper to adopt when speaking of people who are 'not exactly in our set, you know, dear.' 'He's very clever, I've always understood, though hardly the sort of person, of course, one quite cares to mix with in society. He wears such extremely curious hats, and expresses himself so very oddly sometimes. But he's clever in his own way, extremely clever, so people tell me, and full of information about all the ologies. We have a great many of these local celebrities about here, don't you know. There's our postman's a very clever person, too. Why, he writes the most amusing New-Year addresses, all in verse, which he brings round every year when he calls to get his Christmas-box. Geraldine, don't you think you could hunt up some of Briggs's verses to show Mr. Linnell, if he's interested in that kind of thing, you know, dear?'

A faint smile played round the corners of Linnell's mouth at the juxtaposition in Mrs. Maitland's mind of Haviland Dumaresq and the postman poet; but politeness prompted him to say nothing. Comment on his part on such a subject would have been wholly superfluous. He answered not the fool according to her folly. Geraldine, however, could hardly imitate him: she looked up, one flush of sympathetic shame from chin to forehead, and answered quickly: 'No, mother; I don't think I could find them anywhere; and even if I did, I don't think Mr. Linnell would care in the least to see them. You've met the Dumaresqs, Mr. Linnell; so Psyche's been telling me. She says her father's always so glad to come across anybody who's read his books. He's a wonderful old man, so wholly absorbed and swallowed up in his work. He lives for nothing on earth, I do believe, but two things now — Philosophy and Psyche.'

'Two very good things indeed to live for,' Linnell murmured, almost inaudibly. 'I hardly know how he could do better.'

'Yes, he's wasted his life on writing books that were of no earthly use to himself or to anybody,' Mrs. Maitland went on, taking up the thread of her daughter's parable; 'and I've no doubt, now his girl's growing up, he bitterly repents he didn't turn his talents earlier in life to something more useful, that would have brought him in a little money. A gentleman born—for he was once a gentleman—to live contentedly in such a hovel as that! But he was always headstrong, and so's the girl. He never cared for anybody's advice. He was offered a good place under Government once, but he wouldn't take it. He had no time to waste, he said, on making money. He went his own way, and wrote his own useless unsaleable books for his own amusement. And what on earth he lives upon now, nobody hereabouts can ever imagine.'

'His "Philosophy" has had a very small circulation, no doubt,' Linnell ventured to put in apologetically, at the first pause in Mrs. Maitland's flowing river of speech; 'but it has received an immense amount of attention at the hands of all profound thinkers. It gains every day more and more adherents among the most intelligent classes in every country. I believe it will prove to be the philosophy of the future.'

'I don't care much about these "everythings of the future" that we hear such a precious lot of talk about nowadays,' the General put in from the head of the table: 'the music of the future, the politics of the future, the tactics of the future, and all that sort of thing. For my part, I'm quite content to live in the present, where it has pleased a wise Providence to place me, and leave the future to provide its own philosophy, and its own music, and its own tactics, too, whenever it happens to want them. I'm for the present day all round, I am. But I must say I think Dumaresq's a very fine soldierly kind of man in his own way, too; he's been set at his post to hold Philosophy, like a forlorn hope, and he sticks to it bravely, in spite of everything. He thinks he's got his work cut out for him in life. I don't know whether it's good work or bad : I don't understand these things myself : I don't pretend to. In my day soldiers weren't expected to take up philosophy : this wretched examination system that bothers us now hadn't even been invented: we fought and bled and did our duty, and that was all the country asked or wanted of us. It didn't inquire whether Nelson or Wellington had passed an examination in

English literature. But Dumaresq thinks he's called upon by nature or his commanding officer to see this business through to the bitter end, come what may: and he sees it through, right or wrong: and by George, sir, I say, I honour him, too, for it. I've never read one line the fellow's written, and if I did read it, I don't suppose I'd understand a single word of the whole lot, for I've hard enough work to understand what the dickens he's driving at when he's talking, even—let alone when he's writing for the people who can follow him: but I can see he thinks he's sticking to his post, and, hang it all! when a fellow sticks to his post like a brick, if he's only a marine, you know, you can't help admiring him for it.'

'I quite agree with you,' Linnell answered, looking up hastily with most unusual decision. 'Haviland Dumaresq's a very great man, and the way he sticks to his work in life commands one's respect, whatever one may or may not think of his particular opinions.'

'Many of them very questionable,' the Vicar remarked parenthetically.

'But most of them profoundly true and original,' Linnell answered with quiet dignity.

Mrs. Maitland's feminine quickness told her at once that she had started on quite the wrong tack with Linnell, so she made haste diplomatically to retrieve her position.

'Oh, of course, he's a wonderful man in his way,' she said, with conciliating promptitude. 'Just look at the things he's fixed up in the garden for drawing water by hydraulic pressure or something, don't they call it? I know he's a very remarkable man. And what a picturesque, funny little cottage! So you're really sketching it!'

'It *is* picturesque,' Linnell answered, with a fresh return of his engrained dislike to hearing himself or his work talked about. 'The porch is so pretty, all covered with those lovely hanging creepers. I suppose Dumaresq —it seems absurd to speak of so great a man as that as " Mister Dumaresq "—takes care of it himself. I never saw creepers grow better even in Africa.'

'Aren't they just lovely?' Geraldine interposed quickly. 'They always remind me so of dear old Algeria. These passion-flowers I'm wearing came from there. Psyche gave them to me.'

And she handed a stray one from the folds of her dress for Linnell to examine. The painter took it and looked at it closely.

'Miss Dumaresq gave it you!' he said slowly. 'She's very pretty. I should like her to sit to me. In Moorish costume, she'd be the very person for the foreground of that doorway I began at Algiers. You remember the sketch, Miss Maitland; I showed you the study I made for it there: a horseshoe archway in an inner courtyard near the Bab-Azzoun gate, with an Arab girl in indoor dress just stepping out with a tray in her hands among the palms and bananas.' And as he spoke, he thrust the passion-flower without a word into his own button-hole, and pinned it in as if half unconsciously with a pin from the flap of his evening waistcoat.

Geraldine noticed his action with a quiet smile. He had money, she believed; and Psyche liked him.

'She's the very girl for it, Mr. Linnell,' she cried, with unwonted graciousness. Mrs. Maitland by this time had become engaged in conversation by the amiable Vicar. 'Of course I remember your sketch perfectly. You must get her to sit for you. She'd be delighted, I'm sure. Now, do please go to-morrow and ask her.'

'I will,' Linnell answered, anxious once more to escape the subject—for here he was, talking a second time about his own pictures. 'I'm going there, as it happens, to dinner in the evening. I'll take the opportunity to ask her then if she'll give me sittings.'

Geraldine started.

'To dinner to-morrow!' she cried. 'To dinner at the Dumaresqs'! Why, that's quite a new departure for them. I never heard of their asking anybody to dinner before. Lunch sometimes, or afternoon tea; but that's the outside. How very funny! I don't quite understand it.'

'But I do,' Linnell answered. 'I'm going, and the Mansels too. We're all invited.'

Geraldine paused for a moment in surprise. Then she added in an undertone:

'Psyche never said a word of it to me, which is very queer, for I was over there with her the whole afternoon, and she generally tells me everything that happens.'

'She didn't know herself, no doubt,' the

painter replied with a glance at his buttonhole. 'Dumaresq met Mansel and me in the lane about six, and asked us then whether we'd come and dine with them, quite unceremoniously. He seemed rather preoccupied and dreamy this evening. He probably asked us on the spur of the moment, and only went home to tell her afterwards.'

'Probably,' Geraldine answered with a falling face and a slight sigh. 'He seemed preoccupied and dreamy this evening, did he? He's sometimes so. I'm sorry to hear it. But I'm glad you've to dine at Psyche's tomorrow, anyhow. Now I won't let you off, remember. You must paint her in that picture.'

'But how about the Arab costume?' Linnell asked, his usual shyness disappearing for a moment. 'The portrait would be nothing without the haik and the yashmak.'

'I can lend you one,' Geraldine answered

with great promptitude. 'I had it for the Newsomes' charades last season. It'll just suit her—a delicate creamy-white Arab wrap, with the loveliest salmon-pink silky covering.'

'Will you, though?' the painter cried, delighted. 'How very good of you! That's just what I want. The picture shall be painted, you may take my word for it, Miss Maitland. Thank you so much for your kind co-operation.'

At that moment Mrs. Maitland, disengaging herself one second from the Vicar's eye, strained her ears to the utmost to catch their conversation, while politely assenting to her neighbour's views on the best way of dealing with rural pauperism. She couldn't exactly make out what they were saying, but she was sure the conversation was unusually animated. She noted the tone of Linnell's voice, with its obvious note of pleasure and gratification, and she thought she even caught distinctly the words, 'Thank you so much for your kind' something or other.

Later on in the evening, while that safely plain Miss Craigie from the Manor House was putting her stock war-horse through its paces upon the big piano, Mrs. Maitland noticed, to her surprise and pleasure, that Linnell was wearing a passion-flower in his buttonhole.

'Why, what a pretty bouquet!' she said, glancing over at it archly. 'I think I know where you got *that* from, Mr. Linnell.'

Linnell looked down awkwardly at his buttonhole for a second in doubt. It was Psyche's passion-flower, from the creeper on the porch! How should he defend himself? A girl he had only once seen! Then a happy subterfuge flashed across his brain.

'Yes, Miss Maitland gave it me,' he answered, with much boldness. 'It was one of the flowers she was wearing at dinner.'

In his timid anxiety to avoid the imputation of having got it from Psyche, he never saw himself what interpretation Mrs. Maitland must needs put upon his blush and his words. But that astute lady smiled to herself, and remarked inwardly that things seemed really to be coming to a head. Geraldine had given that young man a flower! And the young man for his part had worn it and blushed over it!

As the whole party of visitors walked home together from the Maitlands' that night, Mrs. Mansel turned to the young painter and said, with a meaning look:

'You and Geraldine seemed to get on very well together, Mr. Linnell, in spite of your objection to ladies' society.'

Linnell laughed.

'Her arctic smile thawed a little this evening,' he answered casually. 'Besides, we've found an interest in common. She means to help me in the get-up of a picture for which I hope Miss Dumaresq will give me a sitting.'

At that very moment, in the deserted drawing-room, Mrs. Maitland was saying in a confidential tone to her husband:

'Now, George, remember, when you go up to town next week, you must try to find out at your club the real facts about this young Linnell. Has he money or has he not? That's the question. We ought to make quite sure about his position and prospects before we let things go any further between him and Geraldine.'

'I think he's well off,' the General murmured in reply, beneath his moustaches.

'Think! Oh yes. I think so, too. But where one's daughter's happiness is at stake, you know, George, one oughtn't to rest satisfied with mere thinking: one ought, as the Kirkpatrick said, to "mak sicker." There's some sort of mystery hanging over the young man's head, I fancy. If he has money, why doesn't he marry, and take a country place, and keep his carriage, and hunt the county like other people?'

'Tastes differ,' the General murmured, with philosophic calm, as he lighted his cigar. 'Perhaps the young man doesn't care for hunting.'

'Perhaps not,' Mrs. Maitland replied loftily, curling her upper lip. 'But a young man of means ought to care for hunting: he owes it to society; and if he doesn't care, you may depend upon it, George, he has some good reason of his own for wishing to be singular; and not a very creditable reason, either.'

CHAPTER V.

A MODERN STOIC.

To Psyche Dumaresq it was a matter of much internal questioning next day why on earth her father had invited that charming Mr. Linnell to dinner. A dinner-party, on however humble a scale, at the Wren's Nest was an almost unheard-of novelty. And then, besides, her father had spoken to her somewhat slightingly of Mr. Linnell only the day before yesterday. What could he mean now by this sudden change of front? Why thus incontinently break through all the established rules of that Spartan household, and invite a perfect stranger to a lordly banquet? The thing was really little short of a miracle.

But Psyche would have been even more astonished still if only she could have known the cause of the change in her father's demeanour. It was a chance word dropped by Mansel in the course of conversation, implying that Linnell, for all his studious simplicity of dress and manner, had a good deal more money than he ever pretended to. Within all Psyche's previous experience, a man's possession of money, especially as fixed and certain income, had always to her father been a positive reason for not desiring the honour of his acquaintance. 'I dislike the society of men who don't earn their own living,' he used to say, in his quiet, restrained way. 'The necessity for work is the great humanizer. Those who toil not, neither do they spin, can have but very imperfect sympathies, after all, with those who earn their own livelihood by the sweat of their brow. I'm not prejudiced against money, but I find moneyed folks generally distasteful to me. They may be very nice people in their own circle; but I don't care to let them intersect mine. I feel most at home among my brother-workers.' If Psyche could have known, therefore, the real reason why her father had invited Linnell to dine with them, her astonishment would indeed have reached its zenith.

As it was, however, she contented herself with making the very best preparations the house could afford for the little entertainment that magical evening; and whatever her dinner lacked in delicacies, it certainly more than made up in delicacy; for the flowers were of Psyche's own dainty arrangement, and the fruit was plucked from Psyche's own little garden, and the silk-wrought strip down the centre of the tablecloth had been stitched with that graceful arabesque pattern by Psyche's own pretty and deft little fingers.

When Linnell arrived, he was shown alone into the tiny drawing-room, and he had some minutes to himself to examine its contents before either Psyche or her father came down to receive him. The young man's respect for the author of the 'Encyclopædic Philosophy' gave a profound interest in his eyes to every detail in that small and severely furnished room. Most of the furniture, indeed—at least, whatever had any pretence to rank as a luxury —had been made by Haviland Dumaresq's own hands, and bore the impress of his stern and strictly stoical taste. On the carved oak over-mantel—two plain wooden slabs, supported by pillars of Ionic simplicity—lay an uncut copy of the Japanese translation of Dumaresq's great monumental work, with a framed photograph of a spare face, bearing beneath the simple inscription, 'John Stuart

Mill, to Haviland Dumaresq.' The plain table by the window was covered with pamphlets, letters, and papers: Linnell took up casually the topmost of the lot, and saw at a glance it was a German dissertation ' On Certain Side-Aspects of the Dumaresquian Philosophy,' by two well-known Professors at Bonn and Heidelberg. The next was a controversial religious work by a Polish Archbishop, ' On Rationalistic Ethics, and especially on the Dumaresquian Law of Reciprocity.' By their side lay a paper-covered Italian volume, bearing in its upper left-hand corner the manuscript words ' À Haviland Dumaresq, Hommage de l'Auteur.' Linnell glanced carelessly at the envelopes on the table. One of them was franked with a Chilian stamp; the other had printed across its top in blue letters, ' Bureau of Indian Affairs, Washington.' The gold medal that hung on the wall was the decoration of the

Académie des Sciences at Paris: the diploma rolled up on the bookcase beyond conferred the degree of Doctor of Laws of the University of Vienna. And this was the man, known over the whole civilized world, who toiled hard for his daily bread in that tiny cottage at publishers' hackwork! This was the man whom Mrs. Maitland, in the comfortable villa on the hillside opposite, had complacently classed, in her local ignorance, with the postman poet!

Linnell's heart beat higher as he thought that by unobtrusive means he might yet be able to redress in part this great wrong of our money-grubbing society, and repay directly to Haviland Dumaresq some fraction of the debt which the world owed him. The list from his agent would arrive no doubt to-morrow morning, and Haviland Dumaresq would go to bed next evening (though he knew it not) a couple of hundred pounds or so the richer for the information. And that would be but the beginning of Linnell's work. He would not rest, he declared to himself with fervour, till Haviland Dumaresq, that greatest of thinkers, enjoyed the ease he deserved so richly.

As he turned to examine the books on the shelves—most of them works on philosophy or science, with flattering inscriptions from their authors on the title-page—the door opened, and Psyche entered. Linnell turned round and took her hand gracefully. If he had looked handsome before in his flannels and tennis suit, he looked still handsomer now in evening dress and with a slightly faded blue passion-flower stuck with tender care in his left buttonhole. Psyche's quick eyes recognised that delicate blossom at once.

'Why, that's one of our own, Mr. Linnell,' she said, half startled. 'Did you pick it from the plant at the door as you came in, then?'

Linnell looked down at it with a hesitating glance.

'Well, no,' he said. 'The fact is, Miss Dumaresq, it's a present I've received. I was given it by a lady. Miss Maitland wore it at dinner last night. But,' he added quickly, as Pysche's face fell most unmistakably at that simple announcement, 'she told me it was you who'd given it to her, and I kept it accordingly as a little memento. I would prize anything that came from Haviland Dumaresq's cottage.'

'Let me get you another,' Psyche said, if only to hide her blushes. 'That one's withered.' And she put her hand out of the open window as she spoke, and pulled a blossom from the creeper that looked in at the mullions of the casement.

'Thank you,' Linnell answered, taking it

from her with a certain picturesque awkwardness of manner. 'I shall keep them both.' And he folded the old one reverently as he spoke in a letter he drew from his waistcoat pocket. So much devotion to philosophy is rare; but Haviland Dumaresq was a man in a century—and Psyche was also a girl of a thousand.

They sat and talked with the constrained self-consciousness of youth and maiden for a few minutes, for Linnell was almost as shrinking as Psyche herself, and then Haviland Dumaresq entered to relieve them from their unwilling *tête-à-tête*. He was dressed in a very old and worn evening suit, yet carefully brushed and well preserved: his shirt-front and tie were of the whitest and neatest, and the keen gray eyes and grizzled beard showed even more distinctly than ever, so Linnell thought, the vigour and power of that marvellous brain that lay behind the massive and beetling-browed forehead. He bowed with all his usual stately courtliness to the young painter.

'I hope Psyche has been doing her duty as hostess?' the great man said in that clear and ringing silvery voice of his. 'I've kept you waiting, I'm afraid; but the fact is, I overwrote my time, working at the new chapters on Dissimilation of Verbal Roots, and forgot to dress till twenty past seven. A mind much occupied with internal relations is apt to let external relations slip by unnoticed. You must have observed that yourself, no doubt, in painting.'

'Papa has always to be called two or three times over to every meal,' Psyche put in, laughing. 'And whenever I make a *soufflé* or anything of that sort, I always call him ten minutes beforehand, or else, you know, it's all gone flat before he comes out of his study to eat it.'

Just at that moment the Mansels arrived, and the whole party went in to dinner.

In spite of the bare little dining-room, and the one servant who acted alike as cook and parlour-maid, no dinner was ever prettier or better. It was simple, of course, and of few dishes : you can't expect much from a one-handed menage ; but it bore the impress of a refined household, for all that : it had the nameless charm of perfect gracefulness, which is often wanting to the most sumptuous London entertainments. Linnell felt sure that Psyche had prepared most of it herself beforehand. The pudding was a cold one, and so was the mayonnaise of boiled fish ; so that the one servant had nothing to look after in the kitchen but the clear soup and the one small joint. These details of the hidden domestic management, indeed, Linnell appreciated at once from his old African bachelor experience. But everything was dainty, light, and tempting : even the wine, though but a simple claret, was sound and old and of a choice vintage. Haviland Dumaresq's own conversation with Mrs. Mansel would alone have made any entertainment go off pleasantly. In his stately way, the old man, when once warmed up to talk, could fire off epigram after epigram in quick succession; and when he met a clever woman, who could toss him back the ball as fast as he delivered it, the game between them was well worth watching. Now, Ida Mansel was a clever woman, with just that particular gift of bandying back rapid question and answer which Dumaresq loved as intellectual recreation; and Linnell was content to sit and listen to those two brisk disputants at their mimic conflict for half the evening, with only an occasional aside to Psyche, or a casual remark to his brother-painter. For Haviland Dumaresq's wit was keen and sharp as his thought was profound;

and the contest of words with a pretty woman always stimulated his faculties to their very utmost, and brought out the flashing qualities of his vivid mind in the highest perfection.

Aften dinner, however, when Psyche and Mrs. Mansel had left the table, their conversation fell into a very different channel. A man who meets for the first time in his life one of his pet heroes, likes to make the best of his opportunities by learning as much as he possibly can about the living object of his admiration. Linnell admired Haviland Dumaresq far too profoundly not to be eagerly interested in every detail of his life and history. And Dumaresq, for his part, though he seldom talked of his own affairs, for he was the exact opposite of an egoist—too much absorbed in the world of things to give much of his attention to that solitary unit of humanity, himself —yet broke loose for once, in the presence of one who loved his System, and in a certain grand, impersonal, unostentatious sort of way, gave a brief account of the gradual stages by which that System rose up step after step to full-grown maturity before his mental vision. Linnell listened with all the silent and attentive awe of a disciple as the old man related, bit by bit, how that wonderful conception of the nature of things took gradual concrete shape within him.

'You must have lived a very hard life while you were gathering together the materials for your great work,' the painter ventured to remark at last, as Dumaresq, pausing, raised his glass of claret to his lips to moisten his throat after the graphic recital. 'It must have taken you years and years to collect them.'

The old man gazed across at him with a sharp glance from those keen clear eyes. 'You are right,' he said impressively: 'years and years indeed it took me. For five-and-twenty years I did nothing else but master the infinite mass of detail, the endless facts and principles which went to form the groundwork of the "Encyclopædic Philosophy." When I left Cambridge, now much more than forty years ago, I made up my mind to devote my life without stint or reserve to the prosecution of that single purpose. I meant to spend myself freely on the work. The goal shone already clear as day in the heavens before me; but I knew that in order to work my plan out in all its fulness I must give up at least ten years of my time to the prosecution of multifarious physical researches. The thing grew as such things always necessarily grow. Before I'd arrived at the preliminary mastery of facts which I felt to be indispensable for the development of my clue, I'd given up a full quarter of a century to the mere task of prior preparation. Then I said to myself my tutelage was over: I might begin to live. I wrote my first volume at once, and I also married. My work was done, all but to write it down. I thought I was justified in taking a little care, for the first time in my life, of my own comfort.'

'But if it isn't a rude question,' Linnell cried, all aglow with the reflected fervour of the old man's speech, 'how did you manage to live meanwhile, during the years you gave up to that long preparation?'

Haviland Dumaresq smiled grimly.

'Like a dog,' he answered with simple force: 'like a dog in a kennel. Wherever I was—in London, Paris, Berlin, Washington; for I followed my clue over Europe and America—I took myself a room in the workmen's quarter, as near as possible to the British Museum, or the Bibliothèque Nationale, or the Smithsonian Institute, or wherever else my chief scene of labour lay; and there I lived on bread and cheese and beer, or sometimes less, for years together, while I was working, and collecting, and observing, and arranging. When I look back upon the past, I wonder at it myself. A certain vivid apostolic energy bore me up then. It has evaporated now, and I've become luxurious. But I started in life with exactly fifteen hundred pounds. From the very outset I invested my money, and drawing the interest that accrued each year, I sold out the principal from time to time, to live upon my capital, according as I wanted it. At first, the draughts upon the prime fund were long between; but as years went by and my capital decreased, I had to sell out more and more frequently. Saving and starving the hardest I could starve, sovereign by sovereign, it seemed to slip by me. I gave up the beer; I gave up the cheese; if I could, I would have given up the bread itself, I believe; but in spite of all it still slipped by me. At last, to my utter despair, I found myself one day reduced to my last fifty pounds, while I had still at least five years of solid work staring me in the face unperformed before me. Then I almost gave up all for lost. I fainted in the wilderness. As I sat alone that morning in a fireless room at mid-December, I hid my face in my hands and cried out in my misery. I asked myself why I should continue this task, no man compelling and no man thanking me for it; why I should shut myself out from home and wife and friends and children, and all that other men have always held dearest, for pure love of that vague abstraction, science. I almost gave up out of sheer despondency.'

'And what did you do at last?' Linnell asked, deeply interested.

'For a time I hardly knew what to do. I told my philosophic acquaintances (for I had a few in London) the whole facts of the case; and some of them asked me to come and dine with them, and some of them said it was very hard lines, and some of them proposed to make a fund to help me. But I wouldn't hear of that; even for Philosophy's sake, I was far too proud to accept alms from any man. I nearly broke down with anxiety and despair. Mill made interest for me with your kinsman, old Sir Austen Linnell, who had then charge of the Foreign Office; and Sir Austen tempted me with the offer of a consulship in Peru, which I almost accepted. So brokenhearted was I, that I almost accepted it. Six hundred a year, and collateral advantages. For once in my life the filthy lucre for a moment tempted me. But just at that instant, that critical instant, as luck would have it, an old uncle of mine in America died unexpectedly —a poor man, but he left me his savings, some six hundred pounds all told; and it just pulled me through: it gave me the precise respite I needed. Six hundred pounds was wealth untold to me. I went to work again with redoubled vigour, and spent it every penny for the sake of the System. At the end of five years I sat down a beggar; but with the first volume of my precious book in good black print on my knees before me.'

Linnell drew a long breath.

'To you, Mansel,' he said, turning round to his friend, 'I suppose this is all an old, old story: but as for me, who hear it to-night for the first time, why, it fairly takes my breath away. I call it nothing short of heroic.'

Mansel shook his head.

'It's as new to me, my dear fellow, as to you,' he answered in a low voice. 'Dumaresq has never before this evening told me a single word about it.'.

The old philosopher sighed profoundly.

'What use?' he said, with a gesture of deprecation. 'Why trouble our heads about so small a matter? The universe swarms and teems with worlds around us. We men are but parasites on the warped surface of a tiny satellite of a tenth-rate sun, set in the midst of a boundless cosmos, whose depths are everywhere pregnant with problems. Why should we go out of our way, I wonder, to wring our hands over this fly or that; to discuss the history of any particular individual small parasite among us? The book got done at last; that's the great thing. The world at large may not care to look at it; but there it is, in evidence to this day, the monument of a lifetime, a germ of intellectual yeast cast loose into the fermenting thought of humanity, and slowly but surely assimilating to itself all suitable particles in that vast mass of inane and clashing atoms.'

They paused a moment, and gazed hard at their glasses. Dumaresq's earnestness held them spell-bound. Linnell was the first to break the solemn silence.

'It was a noble life,' he said, 'nobly wasted.'

To their immense astonishment, Haviland Dumaresq made answer energetically :

'Ay, wasted indeed ! There you say true. Utterly, inexpressibly, irretrievably wasted ! And therein lies the sting of the whole story. If I had it all to live over again, of course, I'd waste it as freely a second time—I can't help that : nature has built me so that I must turn perforce to philosophy and science, and spill the wine of my life for the advancement of thought, as naturally as the moth flies into the candle, or the lemming drowns itself in the bays of the Baltic. But wasted it is, as you say, for all that. Now that I'm old, and can look down calmly from the pinnacle of age on the import of life, I see that the world itself is wiser in its generation than any one among its wayward children. The general intelligence, from which all individual intelligence derives itself, runs deeper and truer than any man's personality. The way of the world is the best way in the end, if we only had the sense to see it. *Si jeunesse savait, ou si vieillesse pouvait,* is the sum and substance of all experience. If I had my life to live over again, I'd live it as I've lived it, mistakes and all, I don't doubt, because it's the natural and inevitable outcome of my own perverse and unhappy idiosyncrasy. Philosophy lures me as gin lures drunkards. But if I had to advise any other person, any young man or woman beginning life with high ideals and noble aspirations, I'd say to them without hesitation : " The world is wisest. Go the way of the world and do as the world does. Don't waste your life as I've wasted mine. Work for the common, vulgar, low, personal aims— money, position, fame, power. Those alone are solid. Those alone are substantial. Those alone make your life worth having to yourself. All the rest is empty, empty, empty, empty. Vanity of vanities, all is vanity, except the vain things mean men wisely and meanly strive for." '

There was a long pause, and no one said anything. That awful cry of a bruised and broken spirit took their hearts by surprise. But through the closed door, the murmur of Psyche's voice in the drawing-room could be heard distinctly. The old man listened to it and smiled serenely. The cloud that had brooded over his forehead cleared away. Then he rose, and going to a hanging cupboard above the mantelshelf, took out a small round box, and from it brought forth a little silver-coated pellet.

'It excites my nerves when I talk this way,' he said apologetically, as he washed the medicine down with half a glass of claret. 'I always require something to still my brain after speaking on these purely personal matters—they rouse the glands to unnatural activity. Mansel, will you have another glass of wine ? No ? Then suppose we join your wife and Psyche ?'

CHAPTER VI.

A SLIGHT MISUNDERSTANDING.

LINNELL went home to the Red Lion well content that evening: for Haviland Dumaresq had poured out his full heart to him; and Psyche had given him her faithful promise to sit to him in Arab costume for his projected picture. Not that as yet he was in love with Psyche; love at first sight was alien to the artist's timid and shrinking nature; but he had recognised from the very first moment he saw her that he would be more capable of conceiving a grand passion for that beautiful girl than for any other woman he had ever met in the course of his wanderings. To begin with, was she not Haviland Dumaresq's daughter? and Linnell's reverence for the great thinker, in his solitude and poverty, was so profound and intense that that fact alone prepossessed him immensely from the very first in Psyche's favour. But even had she been the daughter of a Mrs. Maitland or a village innkeeper, Linnell could hardly have helped being interested in the pink-and-white maiden. He had sat and talked with her all the evening long in a convenient corner; he had drawn her out slowly, bit by bit; her shyness and reserve had made him almost forget his own; her innocent pleasure at the attention he paid her had flattered and delighted his sensitive spirit. Though Haviland Dumaresq had honoured him with his confidence, it was of Psyche he thought all the small-hours through; it was Psyche's voice, not the great philosopher's, that rang in his ears as he lay awake and hugged himself; it was Psyche's eyes that made his heart flutter with unwonted excitement through the night-watches.

Linnell was thirty, and at thirty these symptoms come stronger than in early youth. It is then that a man begins to know himself a man : it is then that he begins to recognise and appraise his own effect upon the hearts of women.

He liked Psyche—liked her immensely ; but the really important question was this, Did Psyche like him ? He knew enough about women, of course, by this time, to know that six or seven thousand a year will buy you outright the venal love of half the girls in a London ballroom. He knew that, and he didn't care to invest his money in the unprofitable purchase. The question was, Did Psyche really like him for himself, or could Psyche be made so to like him ? He glanced down uneasily, as he sat in his own arm-chair in the inn room, at his lame leg, or the leg that he still insisted on considering as lame, and asked himself gravely many times over, Would Psyche take him, limp and all included, without the dead make-weight of that hypothetical and unacknowledged fortune? If Psyche would, then well and good: it was an honour for any man to marry Haviland Dumaresq's daughter. But if Psyche wouldn't—— Ha, what a start! As he thought the words to himself, Linnell for the first time realized in his soul how deeply his life had already intertwined itself with Psyche's.

The dream was born but the day before yesterday; and yet even to-day to give it up would cost him a lasting pang of sorrow.

He had understood well what Haviland Dumaresq meant when he said that if he had to advise any young man or woman beginning life he would tell them to go the way of the world, and work for money, position, and power. The great philosopher was a father, after all: he was thinking of Psyche. And for that, Linnell could not really find it in his heart to blame him. The old man had led his own heroic life, in his own heroic self-denying way, for a grand purpose: he had spent himself in the service of thought and humanity. But when he looked at Psyche's beautiful young life—at that pink-and-white rosebud, just opening so sweetly and daintily to the air of heaven—he might well be forgiven for the natural wish to surround her with all possible comfort and luxury. A man may be a Stoic for himself if he likes, no doubt, but no good man can ever be a Stoic for those he loves best—for his wife or his daughter.

There the painter thoroughly sympathized with him. If he married Psyche, it would be because he wished to make her happy: to give her all that money can give: to make life more beautiful and worthy and dear to her. For that, he would gladly fling away everything.

So Linnell could easily forgive the father if he wished Psyche, as the world says, 'to marry well'—to marry money—for, in plain prose, that was what it came to. He could forgive even Haviland Dumaresq himself for that vulgar thought. He could forgive Dumaresq—but not Psyche. If Psyche took him, she must take him for pure, pure love alone. She must never ask if he was rich or poor. She must never inquire into the details of his banking-book. She must fling herself upon him just because she loved him. He wanted in his way to do after the fashion of the Lord of Burleigh. He must be but a landscape-painter, and a village maiden she. On those terms alone would he consent to be loved. And on those terms, too, he said to himself, with a little thrill of delight, Haviland Dumaresq's daughter would be content to love him. If Psyche were made of other mould than that—if Psyche were swayed by vulgar ideals and base self-interest—if Psyche were incapable of devotion like her father's, or of love like his own—then Linnell for his part would have nothing to say to her. It was just because he felt sure something of Haviland Dumaresq's grand self-forgetfulness must run innate in his daughter's veins that the painter believed he could give up his life for her.

So he whispered to himself, as he lay awake that night and thought of Psyche. But at that very moment, at the Wren's Nest, a gray old man, erect and haughty still, but with that dreamy look in his eyes that Linnell had noticed so keenly on their second meeting, stole on tiptoe into the room where his daughter slept, and regarding her long in a strange ecstasy of delight, candle in hand, murmured to himself in low hazy tones: 'She *shall* be rich. She *shall* be happy. She shall have all she wants. She shall live the life I never lived. I see it. I feel it. I know it's coming.—A rich man shall love her. I feel it's coming.—Space swells around me. The walls grow bigger. The world grows wider. The music rings. How glorious it all looks in Psyche's palace! I shall make her happy. I shall guard her and watch over her. She shall never fling her life away, as I flung mine, for vain conceits, for empty shadows. I see the vision. I hear the music. It rings in my ears. It tells me she shall be happy.'

If a medical man could have looked at the great philosopher's eyes just then, he would have needed but little experience to tell you that the silver-coated pellet Haviland Dumaresq had swallowed to calm his nerves the evening before was pure opium. It was thus that nature revenged herself at last for long years of excessive toil and terrible privation.

Next day Psyche was to begin her sittings in the Arab costume. Linnell was up early, and opened his letters from London at the breakfast-table. Among them was one from his agent in town, giving a list of all libraries and institutions in the English-speaking world to which copies of Haviland Dumaresq's great work could be sent by an ardent admirer. The number a little surprised himself: his agent had hunted up two hundred and seventy distinct recipients. The complete series of the 'Encyclopædic Philosophy' was published at three guineas a set: the total would amount, therefore, to £850 10s. He totted up the number on the back of an envelope, and drew a long breath. That was a big sum—much bigger than he expected; but it would make Dumaresq rich for many a long day to come. Eight hundred and fifty was nothing to him.

He took his cheque-book from his portmanteau, and filled in a cheque for that amount offhand. Then he wrote a short note of instruction to his agent; packed up his easel for the morning's work; dropped letter and cheque in the post-box as he passed, and presented himself betimes at the Wren's Nest, with an approving conscience, to fulfil his engagement.

He was glad to think he had done so much to make Psyche and her father both happy. And he was glad, too, in a certain indefinite, half-conscious way, that he'd planned it first for Haviland Dumaresq's own sake, before he even knew of Psyche's existence. Love of philosophy, not love of a girl, had given him the earliest impulse to do that kind and generous action.

It was a happy morning, indeed, for both the young people. Linnell had to pose and drape Psyche, with Geraldine Maitland's friendly assistance—for Geraldine had come round to bring the Arab dress, and remained to perform propriety for the occasion. 'Papa wouldn't come down this morning,' Psyche said, blushing: 'he had one of his very bad headaches to-day. She noticed last night that papa's eyes had that strange far-away, dreamy look about them which, she always observed, was followed soon by a racking headache. He was dreadfully depressed when he got well, too: he'd have a terrible fit of depression to-morrow, she was afraid.' Linnell was politely sorry to hear that; yet too secretly glad at the proximate success of his own device to feel that the depression could be very permanent. It was such an impersonal way of doing a man a benefit—increasing the sale of his book so largely. It would all go in with the yearly account, no doubt; and unless Dumaresq inquired very closely into the sales, he would never even find out the real reason of this apparent leap into sudden popularity. He would only know in a vague and general way that a great many more of his books had been sold this year than in any previous year since their first publication.

'There, that'll do exactly,' he said at last, posing Psyche's head, with a soft silky *haik* thrown lightly across it, a little on one side towards her left shoulder. 'Don't you think so, Miss Maitland? It'll do so. That's absolute perfection. Now you can laugh and talk as much as you like, you know, Miss Dumaresq. Don't suppose it's the same as having your photograph taken. What a painter wants above all is the natural expression. The more you're yourself the more beautiful and graceful the picture will be, of course.'

'What a pretty compliment!' Geraldine Maitland murmured archly. 'You never speak that way to *me*, Mr. Linnell.'

The painter looked down and laughed awkwardly. 'But I've never painted *you*, you know, Miss Maitland,' he answered, rather restrained. 'When I do, I'll prepare a whole quiverful of compliments ready for use beforehand.'

'I understand. Precisely so. But with Psyche, you see, they well out naturally.'

Psyche blushed and smiled at once. 'Don't talk such nonsense, Geraldine,' she said with a bashful air. 'Is this right now, Mr. Linnell, please? Geraldine sets me out of pose by talking.'

Linnell looked up from his easel admiringly. 'Go on making her blush like that as long as you please, Miss Maitland,' he said with a smile, as he outlined her delicate face on his canvas. 'That's just how I want it. Nothing could be more perfect. My Fatma or Mouni's supposed to be caught in the very act of falling in love for the first time. I mean to call it "The Dawn of Love," in fact, and you must try to throw yourself as fully as possible into the spirit of the character, you see, Miss Dumaresq.'

If Linnell had wished to make her blush, indeed, nothing he could have said would have succeeded better. The poor girl flushed so crimson at once from chin to forehead that Linnell took pity upon her, and strove at once to turn the current of the conversation. He shifted the subject to Dumaresq and his work, the adherents his system was gaining on the Continent, and his own profound belief in its ultimate triumph. 'All great things grow slowly,' he said, as he worked away at the dainty curve of those quivering nostrils. 'The Newtonian gravitation was disbelieved for half a century, and Lamarck went blind and poor to his grave without finding one adherent for his evolutionary theories.'

'Papa has many,' Psyche said simply, 'and

those, too, among the greatest and most famous of the time. Even among the people we see here at Petherton, I can always measure their intellect at first sight by observing in what sort of respect they hold my father.'

'Then my intelligence must be of a very high order,' Linnell went on, laughing, 'for I believe nobody on earth ranks Haviland Dumaresq higher than I do. To me he seems far and away the greatest thinker I've ever met or seen or read about.'

'To me, too,' Psyche answered quietly.

The reply startled him by its simple directness. It was so strange that a girl of Psyche's age should have any opinion at all of her own upon such a subject; stranger still that she should venture to express it to another so plainly and openly. There was something of Haviland Dumaresq's own straightforward impersonal truthfulness in this frank avowal of supreme belief on Psyche's part in her father's greatness. Linnell liked her all the better for her frank confidence. 'I'm glad to hear you say so,' he said, 'for one knows that great men are often so much misjudged by their own family. No man, we know, is a hero to his valet. Let him be the profoundest philosopher that ever breathed on earth, and he's oftenest looked upon as Only Papa by his own daughters. But I'm glad to know, too, that the faith is spreading. How many copies, now, have you any idea, are usually sold of the " Encyclopædic Philosophy?"

'Oh, not more than ten or twelve a year,' Psyche answered carelessly, rearranging the drapery upon her shining shoulder.

Linnell started.

'Only ten or twelve a year!' he cried, astonished. 'You don't mean to tell me that's really the case? You must be mistaken! I can't believe it. Only ten or twelve copies a year of the greatest work set forth by any thinker of the present century!'

'Yes,' Psyche answered, in that quiet, resigned, matter-of-fact way she had inherited from her father. 'You see, in England, people read it at the libraries: the great sale's all abroad, papa says, and the book's been translated into all European and Asiatic languages, so people for the most part buy the translations, which practically bring in next to nothing. Then the Americans, of course, who read it so much, read it all in pirated editions. They once sent papa a hundred pounds as compensation; but papa sent the cheque back again at once. He said he wouldn't accept it as a present and a favour from people who ought to pay tenfold as a simple act of natural justice.'

'But I suppose whatever are sold now are all clear profit?' Linnell asked tentatively, with many misgivings, lest he should ask too much, and let out beforehand the secret of this enormous bound into supposed popularity.

'Well, yes,' Psyche answered with some little hesitation. 'I believe they are. I've heard papa say Macmurdo and White have long since covered all expenses, and that every copy sold now is money in pocket.'

Linnell breathed freely once more. Then the £850 10s., for which he had sent off his cheque that morning to his agent would be all clear gain to the poor needy Dumaresq. His brush worked on upon the canvas with unusual vigour. He had never had such a sitter in his life before; he had never felt he was doing himself such justice, nor experienced such a supreme internal consciousness of having been useful to others in his generation.

When the head of the great publishing

house of Macmurdo and White received a cheque for £850 10s., and an order for two hundred and seventy complete sets of 'Dumaresq's Encyclopædic' (as the trade in its recognised shorthand calls it), he raised his eyebrows, sucked in his cheeks, and tapped with his forefinger on the desk of the counting-house.

'It's coming, White,' he said, enchanted. 'I told you it was coming. I knew it was bound to come sooner or later. "Dumaresq's Encyclopædic's" certain to sell in the long-run. There's an order here outright for two hundred and seventy of 'em. Two hundred and seventy's a very big lot. See how many we have ready in cloth, will you, and order the rest to be bound at once from the quires to order. I'm devilish glad we bought the copyright of that book outright from the man —and for a mere song, too. It's paid expenses, I see, these three years back : so that's eight hundred and fifty pounds clear profit for the house on a small transaction.'

For when Psyche Dumaresq mentioned the casual fact that every copy sold of her father's great work was 'money in pocket,' she omitted to add the trifling detail that the pocket in question was Messrs. Macmurdo and White's, worshipful publishers', and not the author's, Haviland Dumaresq's. To anyone who lived in the world of books, indeed, that point would have been the first and most natural to make inquiries about: but the painter, in his eagerness to do a good deed, had never even so much as thought of the possibility that the copyright might not be the author's. All that Linnell had actually accomplished, in fact, by his generous intention was simply to put eight hundred guineas or so into the bursting till of a flourishing firm of London publishers.

'And look here, White,' Mr. Macmurdo

called out as his partner left the room to fulfil the order: 'that poor devil Dumaresq never made much out of the book for his pains. Let's send the man a twenty-pound note as a present!'

Most English publishers would have made it a hundred; and no other trade on earth would have made it anything. But Macmurdo and White are proverbially close-fisted; and the twenty-pound note from that amiable firm was all Haviland Dumaresq ever got out of Charles Linnell's well-meant attempt to benefit the great philosopher. When it arrived at the Wren's Nest, Dumaresq turned to Psyche with a smile and said: 'I may keep that honestly. They must have made it well out of me or they wouldn't send it. Though of course I've no right in the world to a penny. But it's dropped in at the very nick of time. It'll cover the cost of that young man's picture.'

CHAPTER VII.

AT THE UNITED SERVICE.

When General Maitland returned a week later from the Métropole Hotel to High Ash, Petherton, it was with conscious rectitude and the sense of a duty performed that he remarked to his wife :

'Well, Maria, I went to the club, and I've found out all about that painter fellow.'

As a matter of fact, indeed, it was with no small persistence that that gallant soldier had prosecuted his inquiries in London town into the Linnell pedigree.

In the smoking-room of the Senior United Service Club, a few days after his arrival in town, he had chanced to light upon Sir Austen Linnell, the supposed cousin of their Algerian acquaintance. Sir Austen, a cold and reserved man, was very full at the moment of his preparations for going to Egypt, to join Gordon at Khartoum by special invitation. Those were the days of the forlorn hope, while communications up the Nile were yet clear, before the Mahdi's troops had begun to invest the doomed city; and Sir Austen had obtained leave, he said, to accept a call from Gordon himself to form one of his staff in the capital of the threatened, but still unconquered, Soudan. This was the very moment for inquiring, clearly. General Maitland fastened himself upon Sir Austen with avidity, and listened patiently to all his details of the outfit he ought to take for the Upper Nile journey, and of the relative advantages of the rival routes viâ Assouan or Suakim to the heart of Africa. At last Sir Austen paused a little in his narrative; and the General, thinking an appropriate moment had now arrived, managed to remark casually:

'By the way, Linnell, we've a namesake of yours stopping down at Petherton just at present. I wonder whether he and you are any relations.'

Sir Austen's brow gathered slightly.

'A painter fellow?' he asked with a contemptuous intonation.

'Well, he certainly paints,' the General answered, with some faint undercurrent of asperity in his tone, for he didn't quite care to hear a possible son-in-law of the Maitlands of High Ash thus cavalierly described; 'but I'm not sure whether he's a regular artist or only an amateur. I think he paints for amusement chiefly. He seems to be coiny. Do you know anything of him?'

'I've heard of him,' Sir Austen replied curtly, perusing the ceiling.

'His name's Austen Linnell too, by the way,' the General went on with bland suggestiveness. 'Charles Austen Linnell, he calls himself. He must belong to your family, I fancy.'

Sir Austen raised his shoulders almost imperceptibly.

'A' Stuarts are na sib to the king,' he answered oracularly, with the air of a man who desires to close, offhand, an unseasonable discussion. And he tapped the table as he spoke with one impatient forefinger.

But General Maitland, once fairly on the scent, was not thus to be lightly put down. He kept his point well in view, and he meant to make for it, with soldierly instinct, in spite of all obstacles.

'The man has money,' he said, eyeing Sir Austen close and sharp. 'He's a gentleman, you know, and very well educated. He was at Christ Church, I imagine, and he travels in Africa.'

'I dare say he has money,' Sir Austen retorted with a certain show of unwonted petulance, taking up a copy of *Vanity Fair* from the table, and pretending to be vastly interested in the cartoon. 'And I dare say he travels in Africa also. A great many fellows have money nowadays. Some of them make it out of cats'-meat sausages. For my own part, I think a sort of gentlemanly indigence is more of a credential to good society at the present day than any amount of unaccountable money. I know I can never raise any cash myself, however much I want it. Land in Rutland's a drug in the market, to be had for the asking. If your friend wants to rent an ancestral estate, now, on easy terms, on the strength of a singular coincidence in our Christian and surnames, I shall be happy to meet him through my agent any day, with a most equitable arrangement for taking Thorpe Manor. If he chose to live in the house while I'm away in Africa (where those confounded Jews can't get at me anyhow), he might make a great deal of social capital in the county out of the double-barrelled resemblance, and perhaps marry into some good family, which I suppose is the height of the fellow's ambition.' And Sir Austen, laying down the paper once more, and puffing away most vigorously at his cigar, strode off with long strides, and without further explanation vouchsafed, to the secure retreat of the club billiard-room.

His reticence roused General Maitland's curiosity to almost boiling-point.

'A' Stuarts are na sib to the king,' Sir Austen had said; but he had never explicitly denied the relationship. Who could this painter Linnell really be, then; and why should the putative head of his house speak with so evident a mixture of dislike and envy about his supposed fortune? The General was puzzled. He looked around him with a comical air of utter despair, and roped his gray moustache to right and left in sore perplexity.

As he gazed round the room, airing his doubts visibly, his eyes chanced to fall upon old Admiral Rolt, seated on a divan in the far corner, and looking up from his perusal of the *Piccadilly Gazette* with a curious twinkle about his small, fat pigs'-eyes. General Maitland nodded a cursory recognition; and the Admiral, laying down his paper nothing loath, in the midst of a brilliant and vehement leader on the supineness of the service and the wickedness of the Administration, waddled across the room on his short fat legs slowly to meet him.

'You were asking Linnell about that Yankee cousin of his,' he said with his oily, gossipy smile—for the Admiral is the licensed tattle-monger of the Senior United Service. 'Well, if you care to hear it, I know that story well from beginning to end. Seen it all through from the day it was launched. Met my old shipmate, the painter fellow's father, in Boston long ago, when I was cruising about on the North American station, and gave him a lift once to Halifax in the old wooden *Bellerophon*, the one that was broken up after Bosanquet's haul-down, you recollect, when I got my promotion. Knew all his people in Rutland, too, from the time I was a baby; and the lady as well: dear me, dear me, she *was* a clever one! Best hand at a page or a saucy chambermaid I ever saw in my born days; and as full of cunning as Canton is of Chinamen.'

'Then they *are* related?' the General asked cautiously.

'Related!' Who? Linnell and the painter? My dear sir, I believe you. First-cousins,

that's all: own brother's sons: and unless
Sir Austen has a boy of his own before he
dies, you take my word for it, that lame
painter man's the heir to the baronetcy.'

'You don't mean to say so!' the General
cried, surprised.

'Yes, I do, though. That's it. You
may take my word for it. Very few
people nowadays know anything about
the story—blown over long ago, as things
do blow over: and Linnell himself—Sir
Austen, I mean—won't for a moment so
much as acknowledge the relationship. It's
not in the Peerage. Linnell don't allow it
to be put in—he disclaims the connection:
and the lame fellow's a sight too proud and
too quixotic to meddle with the family dirty
linen. He doesn't want to have the whole
bundle dragged to light, and Sir Austen
blackguarding his father and mother in every
house in all London. But if ever Sir Austen

dies, you mark my words, the painter fellow 'll come into Thorpe Manor as sure as my name's John Antony Kolt, sir. It's strictly entailed: property follows the baronetcy in tail male. Linnell's done his very best to break the entail, to my certain knowledge, in order to cut off this Yankee cousin: but it's no go: the law can't manage it. The lame man'll follow him as master at Thorpe to a dead certainty, unless Lady Linnell presents him with an heir to the title beforehand—which isn't likely, seeing that they've been over five years married.'

'But why does Linnell object to acknowledging him?' the General asked curiously.

'Well, it's a precious long story,' the old sailor answered, button-holing his willing listener with great joy—a willing listener was a godsend to the Admiral: 'but I'll tell you all about it in strict confidence, as I know the ins and outs of the whole question from the very beginning. It seems Sir Austen Linnell the elder—you remember him?—the thin old fellow with the cracked voice who was once in the F. O., worse luck! and got us into that precious nasty mess with the Siamese about the Bangkok bombardment—well, that Sir Austen, the present man's father, had a brother Charles, a harum-scarum creature with a handsome face and a wild eye, who was a messmate of mine as midshipman on board the *Cockatrice*. The *Cockatrice* one time was stationed at Plymouth, and there we all fell in with an awfully pretty dancing-girl—one Sally Withers her real name was, I believe, in private circles; but they called her at the theatre, if you please, Miss Violet Fitzgerald. So what must Charlie Linnell and this girl Sally do, by George! but get very thick indeed with one another: so thick at last that there was a jolly row over it, and Sir Austen the eldest, who was then living—not the F. O. man, you understand, but his father again, the Peninsular hero, who died afterwards of the cholera in India—came down to Plymouth and broke the whole thing completely up. He carried off Charlie in disgrace to town, dismissed Miss Sally Violet Fitzgerald to her own profession, spirited her away with her troupe to Australia, and made poor Charlie resign his commission, which he was permitted to do at headquarters on easy terms, to prevent some scandal about a forged leave of absence or something from the Port Admiral.'

'But then this man Linnell the painter isn't——'

'Just you wait and hear. That ain't by any means the end of the story. An old sailor must take his own time to spin his yarn. Well, Charlie, he settled down to a respectable life in town, and was pitchforked by his father into a jolly good berth in the backstairs of the War Office, and grew religious, and forswore the theatre, and took to getting up penny readings, and altogether astonished his friends and acquaintances by developing into a most exemplary member of society. Quite an evolution, as folks say nowadays. Some of us had our doubts about the change, of course, who'd known Charlie in the noisy old days on board the *Cockatrice;* but, bless your heart, we said nothing: we waited to see what 'ud be the end of it all. In time, if you please, Master Charlie announces, to our great surprise, he's going to be married—to a second-cousin of his, twice removed, the daughter of a Dean, too, an excellent match, down at Melbury Cathedral. So in due course the marriage comes off, the Dean officiating, and everybody goes into raptures over the bride, and says how wonderfully Charlie has quieted down, and what an excellent man lay hid so long under his brass buttons and his midshipman's uniform. It was "West African Mission Meeting; Charles Linnell, Esquire, will take the chair at eight precisely." It was "Melbury Soup Kitchen; Charles Linnell, Esquire, Ten Guineas." It was "Loamshire Auxiliary, Charles Linnell, Esquire, President and Treasurer." You never in your life saw such a smooth-faced, clean-shaven, philanthropic, methodistical, mealy-mouthed gentleman. He was the very moral of a blameless ratepayer. But under it all, he was always Charlie.'

'And the painter, I suppose, is a son of this man's and the Dean's daughter?' General Maitland interposed, anxious to get at the pith of the long-winded story.

'Don't you believe it,' the Admiral answered energetically, with a small fat wink. 'The Dean's daughter had one nice little boy, to be sure, whom the present Sir Austen still acknowledges as a sort of cousin: but that's neither here nor there, I tell you: he's a parson in Northumberland now, the Dean's grandson, and nothing at all to do with this present history. About three months after that boy was born, however, what should happen but a party of strolling players comes round to Melbury, where Charlie happened to be stopping at the time with his papa-in-law, the Dean, and accepting hospitality from his revered and right reverend friend, the Bishop. Well, the Dean, who was a good sort of body in his way, was all for converting the actors and actresses; so he invited them in the lump from their penny gaff to a meeting at the Deanery, Charles Linnell, Esquire, the eminent philanthropist, to deliver a nice little fatherly address to them. Charlie made them a most affecting speech, and everything went off as well as could be expected till the very last moment, when, just as they'd finished their weak tea and penny buns, and Charlie was moving away with great dignity from the chair, which he'd filled so beautifully, what should happen but a bold, good-looking player woman, whom he hadn't noticed in a dark corner, gave him a dig in the ribs, and called out to him in a fine broad Irish brogue—she'd played some Irish part when Charlie was stationed on the *Cockatrice* at Plymouth—" Och, Charlie, ohone, sure an' it's yourself's the hoary old hypocrite! Don't ye know me, thin, for your wedded wife, Mistress Linnell, me darlin', fresh back from Australia?" And true enough that's just what she was, as it turned out afterwards: for Charlie'd married Miss Sally Violet quite regularly at Plymouth half a dozen years before.'

' What, bigamy !' the General cried in almost mute surprise.

' Ah, bigamy, if you choose to put an ugly name to it : that's just about the long and short of it. But anyhow, there was a regular burst-up that very evening. In twenty-four hours Charlie had disappeared: the eminent philanthropic gentleman had ceased to exist. Miss Sally Violet, who *was* a clever one, and no mistake, and as handsome a woman as ever I set eyes upon, bar none, had got him straight under her pretty little thumb again : he was just fascinated, clean taken by surprise ; and next week, it was all about over every club in London that Charlie Linnell had eloped with her from Liverpool for somewhere in America, and the Dean's daughter was once more a spinster.'

'What a painful surprise !' the General said constrainedly.

'Painful? You may say so. Poor Mrs. Linnell the Second, the Dean's daughter, nearly cried her wretched little black eyes out. But the family stuck by her like bricks, I must say. Sir Austen the eldest declared he'd never acknowledge Mrs. Linnell the First as

one of the family, and he left what he could to
Mrs. Linnell the Second and her poor little
baby, the parson in Northumberland. Meanwhile, Charlie'd gone off on his own hook to
Boston, you see, with five thousand pounds,
saved from the wreck, in his waistcoat pocket,
unable to come to England again, of course, as
long as he lived, for fear Mr. Dean should
prosecute him for bigamy ; but with that
clever little wife of his, the Sally Violet
creature, ready to make his fortune for him
over again in America. She hadn't been there
but a year and a day, as the old song says,
when this new painter baby appears upon the
scene, the legitimate heir to the Linnells of
Thorpe Manor. Well, clever little Mrs. Sally
Violet, she says, says she to Charlie: "Charlie,
my boy," says she, "you must make money
for the precious baby." "How?" says Charlie.
"A pill," says Sally. "But what the dickens
do I know about pills, my dear?" says

Charlie, flabbergasted. "What's that got to do with the question, stupid?" says sharp Mrs. Sally. "Advertise, advertise, advertise, is the motto! Nothing can be done in this world without advertisements." So she took Charlie's five thousand into her own hands and advertised like winking, all over the shop, till you couldn't go up the White Mountain peak without seeing in letters as big as yourself on every rock, "Use Linnell's Instantaneous Lion Liver Pills." Podophyllin and rhubarb did all the rest, and Charlie died a mild sort of a millionaire at last in a big house in Beacon Street, Boston. This fellow with the game leg inherited the lot—the ballet-girl having predeceased him in the odour of sanctity—but I understand he made over a moiety of the fortune to his half-brother, the parson in Northumberland, Mr. Dean's grandson. He said his father's son was his father's son, acknowledged or unacknowledged, and he for his part would never do another the cruel wrong which the rest of the world would be glad enough to do to himself if they had the opportunity.'

' That was honourable of him, at any rate,' the General said dryly.

' Honourable of him ? Well, yes, I grant you that ; honourable, of course, but confoundedly quixotic. The fellow's all full of this sentimental nonsense, though. He won't lay claim to the heirship to the baronetcy in the Peerage, it seems, because the other son's well known in England, and he won't brand his own half-brother with bastardy, he says, whatever comes of it. His own half-brother, by the way, the parson in Northumberland, though he owes his fortune to him, hates him like poison, and would brand *him* with bastardy or anything else as soon as look at him. And then he's got ridiculous ideas about his money generally : doesn't feel sure

the paternal pills ever did any good in the
world to anybody to speak of, though I believe
they're harmless, quite harmless, and I used
to take them myself for years on the North
American Station, where one needs such
things in the hot season. But this young
fellow has doubts as to their efficacy after all,
it seems, and is sensitive about the way his
money was made : says he holds it in trust
for humanity, or some such high-falutin, new-
fangled nonsense, and would like to earn his
living honestly if he could by his own exer-
tions. Charlie sent him over to be educated
at Oxford (though of course he couldn't come
himself), as he wanted to make an English
gentleman of him. He spends the best part
of his fortune in charity, I believe, encourag-
ing people he thinks should be encouraged, and
pensioning off everybody who suffered in any
way, however remotely, by his father's doings.
He's quite quixotic, in fact—quite quixotic.'

'If he thinks it's right,' the General said quietly—for he believed in duty, like an old-fashioned soldier, and was not ashamed to deal in moral platitudes, 'he ought to stick to it. But,' he added after a short pause, 'if he were to marry any nice girl anywhere, I expect he'd turn out much like all the rest of us.'

'Eh, what's that?' the Admiral cried sharply, peering out of his fat little black eyes like a wide-awake hedgehog. 'Marry a nice girl? Ah, yes, I dare say—if any nice girl can only manage to catch him. But the man's as full of fads and fancies as a schoolgirl. Suspicious, suspicious, suspicious of everybody. Thinks people look down upon him because he's lame. Thinks they look down upon him because his mother was only a ballet-girl. Thinks they look down upon him because his father ran away to America. Thinks they look down upon him because the

Linnells of Thorpe Manor won't acknowledge him. Thinks they look down upon him because his money was made out of pills. Thinks they look down upon him for what he is and for what he isn't, for what they think him and what they don't think him. And all the time, mind you, knows his own worth, and doesn't mean to be caught for nothing: has as keen an idea of the value of his money, as perfect a sense of how much the world runs after seven thousand a year, and as good a notion of his own position as heir-presumptive to an old English baronetcy, as any other man in the three kingdoms. But the Linnells were always unaccountable people—most odd mixtures: and even Charlie, in spite of his high jinks and his bare-faced hypocrisy, was chock-full of all sorts of high-flown notions. They say he loved the ballet-girl right through, like a perfect fool, and was only persuaded to marry the Dean's daughter at last by his father swearing she was dead and buried long ago at Plymouth. When I met him at Boston, years after, in the liver-pill business, there he was, billing and cooing with Miss Sally Violet as fondly as ever, and as madly devoted to this lame boy of theirs as if his mother had been a Duchess's daughter.'

And later in the day, when General Maitland had retired to his own room at the Métropole, the Admiral was button-holing every other flag-officer in the whole club, and remarking, with his little pig's-eyes as wide open as the lids would permit: 'I say, So-and-so, have you heard the latest thing out in society? Maitland's girl's trying to catch that Yankee artist fellow, Linnell's cousin!'

CHAPTER VIII.

GETTING ON.

It must be frankly confessed that Linnell took an unconscionably long time in painting in the figure of that bewitching Arab girl in the foreground of his graceful Algerian picture. He arranged and rearranged the drapery and the pose till Psyche herself was fairly astonished at the exacting requirements of high art. Perhaps he had reasons of his own for being in no hurry over his self-imposed task: at any rate, he loitered lovingly over every touch and every detail, and filled in the minutest points of the flesh-tints with even more than his customary conscientious minuteness. Psyche, too, for her part, seemed to like very well her novel trade of artist's model.

'Are you tired yet?' Linnell asked her more than once, as they sat in the gloom of the bare little dining-room at the Wren's Nest together; and Psyche answered always with a smile of half-childish surprise: 'Oh dear no, Mr. Linnell—not the least in the world. I could sit like this and be painted for ever.'

To say the truth, she had never before known she was so beautiful. Linnell could idealize female heads against any man; and Psyche's pretty head came out on his canvas so glorified by the halo of first love that she hardly recognised her own counterfeit presentment.

'Do you always take so much pains with your sitters?' she asked once, as the painter paused and regarded attentively some shade of expression on her lips and eyebrows.

And Linnell smiled a broad smile as he answered truthfully: 'Not unless I think my sitter very well worth it.'

'And in the East, who do you get to sit for you?' Psyche asked, looking up at him with those big liquid eyes of hers.

'Nobody so well worth painting as you,' the artist answered with a faint touch of his brush on the eye in the picture—he had just managed to catch the very light he wanted in it. 'Dancing-girls mostly, who sit for money, or Nubians sometimes, who don't veil their features. But in Lower Egypt and in Algiers, of course, you can't get most of the respectable women to show you their faces at all for love or money.'

Psyche hesitated for a moment; then she said timidly: 'Nobody has ever painted papa. Don't you think some day there ought to be a portrait of him?'

Linnell started.

'Do you mean to say,' he cried, with a fresh burst of surprise, 'there's no portrait of him at all anywhere in existence?'

'Not even a photograph,' Psyche answered with a faint shake of her pretty head. 'He won't be taken. He doesn't like it. He says a world that won't read his books can't be very anxious to look at his outer features. But I think there ought to be a portrait painted of him somewhere, for all that. I look to the future. In after-ages, surely, people will like to know what so great a man as papa looked like.'

'Then you have no fear for his fame?' Linnell asked, half smiling.

'None at all,' Psyche answered with quiet dignity. 'Of course, Mr. Linnell, I don't pretend to understand his philosophy and all that sort of thing; but I don't think I should be worthy to be my father's daughter if I didn't see that, in spite of the world's neglect and want of appreciation, a man with so grand a character as papa must let his soul go out in books which can never be forgotten.'

'I don't think you would,' Linnell murmured very low. 'And one of the things I like best about you, Psyche, is that you appreciate your father so thoroughly. It shows, as you say, you're not unworthy to be so great a man's daughter.'

He had never called her Psyche before, but he called her so now quite simply and unaffectedly; and Psyche, though it brought the warm blood tingling into her cheek, took no overt notice of the bold breach of conventional etiquette. She preferred that Linnell should call her so, unasked, rather than formally ask for leave to use the more familiar form in addressing her.

'Papa would make a splendid portrait, too,' she said wistfully, after a moment's pause.

'He would,' Linnell assented. 'I never in

my life saw a nobler head. If only somebody could be got somewhere who was good enough to do it.'

'Wouldn't you care to try?' Psyche asked with an outburst.

Linnell hesitated.

'It isn't my line,' he said. 'I can manage grace and delicate beauty, I know, but not that rugged masculine grandeur. I'm afraid I should fail to do my sitter justice.'

'Oh, I don't think so at all,' Psyche cried with some warmth. 'You appreciate papa. You admire him. You understand him. You recognise the meaning of the lines in his face. I think, myself, nobody could do it as well as you could.' And she looked up at him almost pleadingly.

'You really mean it?' Linnell exclaimed, brightening up. She was but an inexperienced country girl, yet her opinion of his art gave him more profound self-confidence than Sydney Colvin's or Comyns Carr's could possibly have done. He needed encouragement and the frank note of youthful certainty. No art critic so cocksure as a girl in her teens. 'If you think I could do it,' he went on after a pause, still working hard at the light in the left eye, 'I should be proud to try my inexperienced hand at it. I should go down to posterity, in that case, if for nothing else, at least as the painter of the only genuine and authentic portrait of Haviland Dumaresq.'

'You share my enthusiasm,' Psyche said with a smile.

'I do,' the painter answered, looking over at her intently. 'And, indeed, I can sympathize with your enthusiasm doubly. In the first place, I admire your father immensely; and in the second place'—he paused for a moment, then he added reverently—'I had a mother myself once. Nothing that anybody could ever have said would have seemed to me too much to say about my dear mother.'

'Did you ever paint *her?*' Psyche asked, with a quietly sympathetic tinge in her voice.

Linnell shook his head.

'Oh no,' he said. 'She died before I was old enough to paint at all. But,' he added after a pause, in his most hesitating tone, 'I've a little miniature of her here, if you'd like to see it.'

'I should like it very much,' Psyche said softly. Nothings! nothings! yet, oh, how full of meaning when sweet seventeen says them, with pursed-up lips and blushing cheeks, to admiring thirty.

The painter put his hand inside the breast of his coat and drew out a miniature in a small gold frame, hung round his neck by a black silk ribbon. He handed it to Psyche. The girl gazed close at it long and hard. It was the portrait of a graceful, gracious, gentle old lady, her smooth white hair surmounted by a dainty lace head-dress, and her soft eyes, so like Linnell's own, instinct with a kindly care and sweetness. Yet there was power, too, rare intellectual power, in the ample dome of that tall white forehead; and strength of will, most unlike her son's, stood confessed in the firm chin and the marked contour of the old lady's cheeks. It must surely have been from 'Charlie'—that scapegrace 'Charlie'— that Linnell inherited the weaker half of his nature: in the mother's traits, as set forth by the miniature, there showed no passing line of mental or moral weakness.

'She must have been a very great lady indeed,' Psyche cried, looking close at it.

'Oh no; not at all. She was only a singer —a public singer,' Linnell answered truthfully. 'But she sang as I never heard any other woman sing in all my days ; and she lived a life of pure unselfishness.'

'Tell me about her,' Psyche said simply.

Her pretty sympathy touched the painter's sensitive nature to the core. His eyes brimmed full, and his hand trembled on the lashes of the face in the picture, but he pretended to go on with it still unabashed.

'I can't tell you much,' he said, trying hard to conceal his emotion from his sitter; 'but I can tell you a little. She was a grand soul. I owe to her whatever there may be of good, if any, within me.'

'An American, I suppose?' Psyche went on musingly, as she read the name and date in the corner, 'Boston, 1870.'

'No, not an American ; thank heaven! not that—a Devonshire girl : true Briton to the bone. She was proud of Devonshire, and she loved it always. But she went away to America with my father of her own accord in

her effort to redress a great wrong—a great
wrong my father had unwittingly been forced,
by the cruelty and treachery of others, into
inflicting unawares on an innocent woman—a
woman who hated her, and for whom she
would willingly have sacrificed everything.
I can't tell you the whole story—at least, not
now. Perhaps——' And he paused. Then
he added more slowly : ' No, no ; no, never.
But I can tell you this much in general terms:
my father had been deceived by *his* father—a
wicked old man, my mother said, and my
mother was a woman to be believed implicitly
—my father had been deceived by a terrible
lie into inflicting this cruel and irreparable
wrong upon that other woman and a helpless
child of hers. My mother, who already had
suffered bitterly at his hands—for my father
was a very weak man, though kind and well-
meaning—my mother found it out, and
determined to make what reparation was

possible to her for that irretrievable evil. She never thought of herself. She never even vindicated her own position. She stole away to America, and was as if she were dead; there she toiled and slaved, and built up a livelihood for us in a strange way, and wished that half of all she had earned should belong in the end to that other woman and her innocent child; the woman that hated her. Through good report and evil report she worked on still; she kept my father straight, as no other woman could ever have kept him; she brought me up tenderly and well; and when she died, she left it to me as a sacred legacy to undo as far as in me lay the evil my grandfather and father had wrought between them: one by his wickedness, the other by his weakness. I don't suppose you can understand altogether what I mean; but I dare say you can understand enough to know why I loved and revered and adored my mother.'

'I can understand all, I think,' Psyche murmured low; 'and I don't know why I should be afraid to say so.' With any other woman, the avowal might have sounded unwomanly; with Psyche, girt round in her perfect innocence, it sounded but the natural and simple voice of human sympathy.

Events take their colour from the mind that sees them. There are no such things as facts; there are only impressions. The story old Admiral Rolt had bluntly blurted out at the Senior United Service to General Maitland was the self-same story that Linnell, in his delicate, obscure half-hints, had faintly shadowed forth that day to Psyche; only the mode of regarding the events differed. Between the two, each mind must make its choice for itself. To the pure all things are pure; and to Admiral Rolt the singer of beautiful songs, and the mother that Linnell so loved and revered, envisaged herself only as a common music-hall ballet-girl. How far the scene at the Deanery and the Irish brogue were embellishments of the Admiral's own fertile genius, nobody now living could probably say. On the Admiral's tongue no story lost for want of amplification. Perhaps the truth lay somewhere between the two extremes; but Linnell's was at least the nobler version, and bespoke the nobler mind at the back of it.

They paused for a moment or two in utter silence. Then Linnell spoke again.

'Why do I make you the confidante of this little family episode?' he asked dreamily.

'I suppose,' Psyche answered, looking up at him with something of her father's bold, open look, 'because you knew you were sure of finding friendly sympathy.'

Their eyes met, and then fell suddenly. A strange tremor ran through Linnell's nerves. Was this indeed in very truth that woman who could love him for his own soul, apart from filthy lucre and everything else of the earth, earthy?

He looked up again, and, hasting to change the conversation, asked of a sudden:

'How can I get your father to sit for me, I wonder?'

He was afraid to trust his own heart any further.

Psyche's eyes came back from infinity with a start.

'Oh, he'd never *sit!*' she cried. 'You can't do it that way. We must make up some plan to let you see him while you pretend to be painting something else, and he doesn't suspect it. You must get your studies for it while he knows nothing about it.'

'He might come in here while I paint you,' Linnell suggested with faint indecision, 'and then I could put one canvas behind another.'

A slight cloud came over Psyche's brow. It was so much nicer to be painted *tête-à-tête* with only an occasional discreet irruption from Geraldine Maitland, who sat for the most part reading French novels on the tiny grass plot outside the open window.

'I think,' she said, after a slight pause, 'we might manage to concoct some better plot with Geraldine.'

There's nothing on earth to bind two young people together at a critical stage like concocting a plot. Before that surreptitious portrait of Haviland Dumaresq was half finished—the old man being engaged in conversation outside by Geraldine, while Linnell within caught his features rapidly—the painter and Psyche felt quite at home with one another, and Psyche herself, though not prone to love affairs, began almost to suspect that Mr. Linnell must really and truly be thinking of proposing to her. And if he did—well, Psyche had her own ideas about her answer.

CHAPTER IX.

FOR STRATEGIC REASONS.

'GEORGE!' Mrs. Maitland remarked abruptly to her husband one evening, a few weeks later, as they sat by themselves, towards the small-hours, in the High Ash drawing-room, 'we must put our foot down without delay about Geraldine and this flighty girl of poor crazy old Dumaresq's.'

The General wavered. He was an old soldier, and he knew that when your commanding officer gives you a definite order, your duty is to obey, and not to ask for reasons or explanations. Where Geraldine was in question, however, discipline tottered, and the General ventured to temporize somewhat. He salved his conscience—his military conscience—by pretending not quite to understand his wife.

'Put our foot down how?' he managed to ask, prevaricating.

Mrs. Maitland, however, was not the sort of woman to stand prevarication.

'You know perfectly well what I mean,' she answered, bridling up, 'so don't make-believe, George, you haven't observed it yourself. Don't look down at the carpet, like a fool, like that. You've seen as well as I have all this that's going on every day between them. Geraldine's behaved disgracefully—simply disgracefully. Knowing very well we had an eye ourselves upon that young man Linnell for her—a most eligible match, as you found out in London—instead of aiding and abetting us in our proper designs for her own happiness, what must she go and do but try her very hardest to fling him straight at the head of that bread-and-butter miss of poor crazy old Dumaresq's? And not only that, but, what's worse than all, she's helped on the affair, against her own hand, by actually going and playing gooseberry for them.'

'But what can we do?' the General remarked helplessly. 'A girl of Geraldine's spirit——'

His commanding officer crushed him ruthlessly.

'A girl of Geraldine's spirit!' she repeated with scorn. 'You call yourself a soldier! Why, George, I'm ashamed of you! Do you mean to tell me you're afraid of your own daughter? We must put our foot down. That's the long and the short of it!'

'How?' the General repeated once more with a shudder. It went against the grain with him to repress Geraldine.

'There are no two ways about it,' Mrs. Maitland went on, waving her closed fan like a marshal's baton before her. 'Look the thing plainly in the face, for once in your life, George. She *must* get married, and we *must* marry her. Last year she refused that rich young Yankee at Algiers. This year she's flung away her one chance of this well-to-do painter man. She's getting on, and wasting opportunities. There's Gordon's got into difficulties at Aldershot again: and Hugh, well, Hugh's failed for everything: and the boys at Winchester are coming on fast: and unless Geraldine marries, I'm sure I don't know what on earth we're ever to do for ourselves about her.'

'Well, what do you want me to *do*?' the General asked submissively. A soldier mayn't like it, but a soldier must always obey orders.

'Do? Why, speak to her plainly to-morrow,' Mrs. Maitland said with quiet emphasis. 'Tell her she mustn't go round any more wasting her time with these half-and-half Dumaresqs.'

'Dumaresq's a gentleman,' the General said stoutly.

'Was one, I dare say. But he's allowed himself to sink. And, anyhow, we can't let Geraldine aid and abet him in angling to catch this poor young Linnell for his daughter Psyche, or whatever else he calls the pink-and-white young woman. It's a duty we owe to Mr. Linnell himself to protect him from such unblushing and disgraceful fortune-hunting. The girl's unfitted to be a rich man's wife. Depend upon it, it's always unwise to raise such people out of their natural sphere. You must speak to Geraldine yourself to-morrow, George, and speak firmly.'

The General winced. But he knew his place.

'Very well, Maria,' he answered without a murmur.

He would have saluted as he spoke had Mrs. Maitland and military duty compelled the performance of that additional courtesy.

So next morning after breakfast, with many misgivings, the General drew his daughter gently into his study, and begged her in set form to abstain in future, for her mother's sake, from visiting the Dumaresqs.

Geraldine heard him out in perfect composure.

'Is that all, papa?' she asked at last, as the General finished with trembling lips.

'That's all, Geraldine.'

He said it piteously.

'Very well, papa,' Geraldine answered, holding herself very tall and erect, with one hand on the table. 'I know what it means. Mamma asked you to speak to me about it. Mamma thinks Mr. Linnell might marry me. There mamma's mistaken. Mr. Linnell doesn't mean to ask me, and even if he did, I don't mean to take him.'

'You don't?'

'No, papa; I don't. So that's the long and short of it. I don't love him, and I won't marry him. He may be as rich as Crœsus, but I won't marry him. More than that: he's in love with Psyche; and Psyche I think's in love with him. They want my help in the matter very badly; and unless somebody takes their future in hand and makes the running very easy for them, I'm afraid Mr. Linnell will never summon up courage to propose to Psyche. He's so dreadfully shy and reserved and nervous.'

'So you mean to go there still, my child, in spite of what I say to you?'

Geraldine hesitated.

'Father dear,' she cried, putting her graceful arms round the old man's neck tenderly,

'I love you very, very much; but I can't bear not to help poor dear lonely Psyche.'

The General's courage, which was all physical, oozed out like Bob Acres's at the palms of his hands. This was not being firm; but he couldn't help it. His daughter's attitude had his sincerest sympathy. The commanding officer might go and be hanged. Still, he temporized.

'Geraldine,' he said softly, bending her head to his, 'promise me at least you won't go to-day. Your mother 'll be so annoyed with me if you go to-day. Promise me to stop at home and——'

'And protect you, you old dear!' She reflected a moment. 'Well, yes; I'll stop at home just this once, if only to keep you out of trouble. Give Mr. Linnell a chance of speaking if he really wants to. Though what on earth poor Psyche'll do without me I'm sure I don't know. She's expecting me to-day. She counts on my coming. I'll have to write and tell her I can't come; and Psyche's so quick, I'm afraid she'll guess exactly why I can't get round this morning to help her.'

The General breathed more freely once more.

'There's a dear girl,' he said, stroking her hair gently. 'Your mother would have been awfully annoyed if you'd gone. She thinks it's wrong of you to encourage young Linnell in his flirtation with that girl. Though I quite agree with you, Geraldine, my dear, that if you don't love a man, you oughtn't to marry him. Only—it'd be a very great comfort to us both, you know, my dear, if only you could manage ever to love a man who was in a position to keep you as we've always kept you.'

'I don't know how it is,' Geraldine answered reflectively. 'I suppose it's original sin or the natural perversity of human nature coming out in my case; but I never *do* like men with money, and I always fall in love with men without a ha'penny. But, there; I've no time to discuss the abstract question with you now. I must run up at once and write this note to poor Psyche.'

CHAPTER X.

AS BETWEEN GENTLEMEN.

THAT same morning Linnell sat in his own room at the Red Lion, with a letter of Sir Austen's lying open before him, and a look of sad perplexity gathering slowly upon his puckered brow. It was natural, perhaps, that Sir Austen should wish to settle the question once for all before leaving England: natural, too, that Sir Austen should look at the whole matter purely from the point of view of Frank Linnell, 'the parson in Northumberland,' whom alone he had been sedulously taught from his childhood upward to consider as his cousin, though the law would have nothing to do with countenancing their unacknowledged relationship. And yet Linnell was distinctly annoyed. The tone of the letter was anything but a pleasant one. 'Sir Austen Linnell presents his compliments'—what a studiously rude way of addressing his own first-cousin, his next of kin, his nearest relative, the heir to the baronetcy! Linnell took up his pen and, biting his lip, proceeded at once, as was his invariable wont, to answer offhand the unpleasant communication.

'Mr. C. A. Linnell presents his compliments——' No, no; as he wrote, he remembered with a blush that verse of Shelley's, 'Let scorn be not repaid with scorn;' and rising superior to the vulgar desire to equal an adversary in rudeness and disrespect, he crumpled up the half-written sheet in his hands, and began again upon a fresh page in more cousinly fashion :

'DEAR SIR AUSTEN,

'I can readily understand that your friendship and affection for my half-brother Frank Linnell should prompt you to write to me on the unfortunate question of the succession to the title before leaving England. The subject, I need hardly say, is a painful one to every one of us: to none of us more so, I feel sure, than to myself. But as you are the first to open communications upon it, there can be no reason on earth why I should not answer your queries frankly and straightforwardly without reserve. In the first place, then, during your lifetime I can promise you that I will not overtly or covertly lay claim in any way to the heirship to the title and estates of the baronetcy. In the second place, during my brother Frank's lifetime I will not lay claim to the baronetcy itself, should it ever fall to me, thereby implying any slight upon him or upon my father's memory. But, in the third place, I will not, on the other hand, permit him to put any such slight upon me or upon those whose memory is very dear to me by claiming it for himself without any real legal title. Such a course, I think, would imply a dishonour to one whom I revere more than any other person I have ever met with. I hope this arrangement, by which I practically waive my own rights and my place in the family during my brother's life and yours, will prove satisfactory and pleasing to both of you.—With my best wishes for your success in your African trip, I am ever

'Your sincere friend and cousin,

'CHARLES AUSTEN LINNELL.'

He wrote it at one burst. And when he had written it he felt all the lighter for it.

He had an appointment that morning at eleven with Psyche, and as soon as the letter was off his mind he went round to the Wren's Nest trembling with suppressed excitement. In his hand he carried the water-colour sketch of the cottage, now completed and framed, for presentation to Psyche. If he saw her alone, he had it half in his mind to ask her that morning whether or not she would be his for ever. Those lines from the Lord of Burleigh kept ringing in his ears—

> 'If my heart by signs can tell,
> Maiden, I have watched thee daily,
> And I think thou lov'st me well.'

Surely, surely, Psyche loved him. So timid and sensitive a man as himself could not have been mistaken in his interpretation of her frank confidence and her crimson blushes.

He was not destined to find Psyche alone, however. As he entered, Haviland Dumaresq met him in the garden, tearing up a note from Geraldine to his daughter. The note had annoyed him, if so placid a man could ever be said to display annoyance. It mentioned merely 'in great haste' that Geraldine would not be able to come round and assist at the sitting to-day, as mamma was dreadfully angry about something, and poor papa wanted her to stop and break the brunt of the enemy's assault for him. Psyche knew in a moment what the letter meant—she had old experience of Mrs. Maitland's fancies—and handed it without a word of explanation to her father. The great philosopher took it and read it. 'All women are alike, my child,' he said philosophically, crumpling the paper up in his hand: 'they insist upon making mountains out of molehills. And there's nothing about men that irritates them more than our perverse male habit of seeing the molehill, in spite of all they may say to magnify it, in merely its own proper proportions. A due sense of social perspective is counted to our sex for moral obliquity. Go in and get yourself ready, Psyche. I'll wait out here and talk to Mr. Linnell for you.'

When Linnell arrived upon the scene, picture in hand, a few minutes later, Haviland Dumaresq, straight and proud as ever, stepped forward to meet him, tearing up the peccant letter into shreds as he went, and scattering its fragments over his own dearly-loved and neatly-kept flower-beds. He saw what the water-colour was at a glance, and taking the painter's hand in his own, with some chilliness in his manner—for it was clear this young man was seeing quite too much of Psyche, when even Mrs. Maitland noticed it and animadverted upon it—he said with the air of a patron of art, not magniloquently at all, but simply and naturally : ' So you've brought home the sketch. We shall be glad to have it.'

Linnell was taken aback by the quiet business assumption implied in his tone, and looking up quickly into the great man's face—for to him Dumaresq was always great, in whatever surroundings—he stammered out in answer, with a certain shamefaced awkwardness: 'I hoped Miss Psyche might be good enough to accept it from me.'

The philosopher glanced back at him with an inquiring gaze. 'Oh no,' he said coldly, examining the picture with a critical eye. 'This sketch was a commission. I asked you to do it for us. You must let me pay you whatever's proper for it.'

Linnell hardly knew whether to feel more amused or annoyed. Dumaresq, he felt sure, must have received his eight hundred guineas already, and he inclined to assume a princely air of patronage to art on the strength of this sudden access of unwonted opulence. Still, even though the money came directly out of his own pocket, he couldn't bear to sell the sketch of Haviland Dumaresq's cottage to the great philosopher—and to Psyche's father.

'It was a labour of love,' he ventured to say with quiet persistence, in spite of Dumaresq's chilling austerity. 'I did it with more than my usual success, I dare to think, because I was inspired by the importance of the subject, and because I thought you would allow me to present it as a memento to Miss Dumaresq. Besides, you know, it's only right she should accept it from me in return for the trouble I've given her about the other painting. Your daughter has put me under great obligations in permitting me to paint her in the foreground of my Academy picture.'

Dumaresq drew himself up even more stiffly than before.

'My daughter,' he said with a very cold and clear intonation, 'is not, as you seem to think, a professional model. She doesn't expect payment in any way for her services.

If her face is of use to you for the purposes of art, we are both of us glad that art should be the richer for it. A beautiful face is a gift of nature, intended for the common good of humanity: a beautiful picture makes the world so much the better for its existence and its beauty. I would not grudge to art the power to multiply beautiful faces—and Psyche's *is* beautiful—to the utmost of its ability. But you must tell me how much I owe you for this sketch, all the same. It's unbecoming the dignity both of art and of philosophy that an artist and a philosopher should haggle together in the matter of price over such a subject.'

Linnell bowed his head in silent acquiescence. After all, he thought to himself, fifty pounds was not worth fighting about; the money in the end came out of his own pocket. And he didn't wish to offend Psyche's father. In a very little time, perhaps—and his heart beat high—it would matter very little which of them had the money, himself or Psyche.

'If you insist upon it, Mr. Dumaresq,' he said at last with a painful effort, 'though it's a great disappointment to me not to be permitted to offer the picture as a present to your daughter, we'll make it, as you prefer, a matter of business. Suppose then, by way of putting a price upon it, we set down the value at twenty guineas.'

Haviland Dumaresq drew a long breath. This was eleven pounds more than his utmost imagination. But he was far too proud to show his surprise openly. He had Macmurdo and White's twenty-pound note that moment in his pocket. He drew it forth with calm determination, like a man to whom twenty pounds is less than nothing, and, adding to it a sovereign from his purse, laid it simply in the painter's palm. The coin burned into

Linnell's hand, for he, too, was proud—proud and sensitive. He had never been paid so brusquely in his life before, and the hard, matter-of-fact mode of the business transaction made him for the very first time feel ashamed of his profession. But he gave no outward sign, any more than Dumaresq himself had done, of his internal feelings. He thrust the money loose with his hand into his trousers pocket, and muttering something inarticulate about the lights being bad to-day for painting, begged to be excused from going on with the portrait. Then he turned around, and walked slowly out of the garden gate, and up on to the Downs, where he wandered long alone reflecting bitterly with himself that great men, when you come to see them at close quarters, fail often in the end to correspond with one's preconceived opinion of their innate greatness. It must be always so. They give the people of their best, of course; and the people judge the whole by the sample.

As for poor Psyche, who, waiting in the drawing-room, had heard this brief colloquy through the open window, she went upstairs to her own bedroom, and, flinging herself on the bed in her Arab costume, cried her poor little eyes out to think that papa should behave so harshly to that dear Mr. Linnell, who admired him so much, and would give his life almost to do anything for either of them.

For Psyche, too, in her clear girlish way, was quite certain that Linnell loved her.

CHAPTER XI.

FOOL'S PARADISE.

Haviland Dumaresq, left to himself in the garden, paced up and down the narrow gravel walk, and turned over in his mind all these things seriously. Could it be that Mrs. Maitland was right, after all? Was the painter man really coming after Psyche?

Women are lynx-eyed in matters of emotional expression, he reflected to himself in his generalizing way: in that they resemble savages and the lower animals. Yes, and the women of the inferior intellectual grades, like Mrs. Maitland, are more lynx-eyed as a rule even than others: the lower the grade, the more developed the instinctive perceptive faculty. Their intuitions stand them in stead of reason. And such intuitions seldom err. No doubt she was right: no doubt she was right. The young man wanted to marry Psyche.

But in that case what ought he himself, as a father, to do? The young man had probably neither money nor position.

In any other relation of life, indeed, Haviland Dumaresq would never have thought for one moment of inquiring about either of those adventitious circumstances. And he would have regarded their possession to a great extent as a positive disadvantage to the man who was cumbered with them. Money, he would have said, was a bar to exertion : position was antagonistic to wide human sympathies. Those men best know the universe in which they live, those men best love their kind and all other kinds, who earn their own bread by the sweat of their brow, and who have felt the keen spur and common bond of hunger. So, as recommendations to a man in the abstract, poverty and insignificance were far more important in Haviland Dumaresq's mind than money and position.

But where Psyche was concerned things seemed quite otherwise. The old philosopher had wasted his own life in the way he liked best, in obedience to the imperious demands of his own inmost and highest nature; but he wasn't going to let that beautiful girl of his waste hers in the same foolish spendthrift manner: she should profit, he whispered to himself fondly, by her father's hard and dearly-bought experience. For his own part, Haviland Dumaresq would not have taken from Charles Linnell a twenty-guinea picture; but for Psyche he was ready to take from the first comer ten thousand a year, and a title, and a castle, and a place in the peerage, and anything else of vulgar estimation that the world, the mere wealthy commonplace world, could give him. He was prepared to debase himself to Mrs. Maitland's level.

A twenty-guinea picture indeed ! The young man seemed to ask twenty guineas for it as if money were water. Nay, he seemed actually to be putting his price very low, as a matter of friendship to a special purchaser— and if so, Haviland Dumaresq felt he ought certainly to resent the uncalled-for liberty, for what right had the fellow to presume upon doing him a favour when he didn't even so much as wish it ? But, setting that aside, and thinking only of Psyche, if the young man could really get twenty guineas—or more— for a mere casual water-colour sketch, mightn't the matter be worth inquiring into, after all ? Mightn't he be a rising and well-to-do artist ? Haviland Dumaresq hated himself for the unworthy thought; but for Psyche's sake he must hunt up something about this twenty-guinea painter fellow.

After all, painters are often somebodies—even as the world judges, often somebodies. A painter—Heaven forgive him for so low a point of view of an ennobling art—a painter may rise to be P.R.A. at last, and gain a knighthood, and be petted and admired, and earn lots of money, and lose his own soul—whatever was highest and purest and best within him—and make his wife be called My Lady, and give her all that money can buy of place and pleasure, and drive her out in the Park in a carriage with footmen, and take her to Court, like an African savage, bedizened with powder and paint and ostrich-feathers. Pah! the lowness, the meanness, the vulgarity, the barbarism of it! But for Psyche! A painter may often be a really rich man. Why, yes, he was really and truly sinking to the abject level of a Mrs. Maitland.

Mrs. Maitland! An idea! The note! The note! What made Mrs. Maitland angry about Psyche? Not merely because Psyche had got an admirer. Clearly, she must have thought that Psyche was setting her cap—as she would call it in her own hideous match-making dialect—at this twenty-guinea painter fellow. But if so, that meant, as Haviland Dumaresq instinctively knew, that Mrs. Maitland wanted the painter fellow herself for Geraldine. And surely Mrs. Maitland wouldn't want the young man unless she was sure he was a good investment. The Maitlands lived up to the very last penny of the General's pay and the very last farthing of Mrs. Maitland's small fortune. The boys were expensive: one in the army; two at Sandhurst or Marlborough; and one who, as his mother ingeniously observed, had 'failed for everything,' and must now be shipped off to try his fortune in New Zealand or Manitoba. It was positively necessary, as the Maitlands would put it, that Geraldine should marry a man with money. And a man with money enough for Geraldine Maitland would presumably have money enough for his Psyche also.

Haviland Dumaresq paced up and down the garden-walk, revolving these things long in his own troubled mind, turning them all over this way and that, and unable to arrive at any decision about them. At last, wearied out with his own anxious thought, he sat down on the bench under the gnarled old apple-tree, and taking from his waistcoat pocket that small cardboard box with the silver-coated pellets, raised one of them mechanically to his trembling lips to calm his nerves from the tempest that possessed them.

Psyche's happiness! Ay, Psyche's happiness! It was no less than Psyche's happiness that was at stake. And to Haviland Dumaresq, now that the 'Encyclopædic Philosophy' was well off his hands, and launched upon posterity, the universe consisted mainly of Psyche. Talk about the anthropocentric fallacy indeed! Who had done more to dispel that illusion than Haviland Dumaresq? Who had shown more clearly than he that instead of the universe revolving about man as its fixed point and centre, man was but a single unimportant species, on the wrinkled surface of an unimportant satellite, attached by gravity to an unimportant sun—the final product of arrested radiant energy on the outer crust of an insignificant speck in boundless space? And yet, when it came to the actual internal world, was it not also a fact that for Haviland Dumaresq the central point in all the universe was Psyche, Psyche, Psyche,

14—2

Psyche? and that around her as primary all the suns and constellations circled in their orbits like obedient servants? Was it not for her that the cosmos itself loosed the bands of Orion and shed the sweet influences of the Pleiades through long leagues of space upon her nightly dreams?

He was roused from his reverie by a footstep on the gravel path outside; not the footstep of a labourer slouching by to work on the allotments beyond—Haviland Dumaresq, in his inferential fashion, knew it at once for the firm and even tread of a gentleman. The Loamshire hinds loiter about like the half-emancipated serfs they still are, he said to himself quietly: this is the step of a freeman born, who walks the soil of England as if it belonged to him. And sure enough, raising his eyes across the hedge, he saw before him Reginald Mansel.

'Ha, Mansel,' he cried, beckoning his

painter neighbour to turn aside into the garden, 'this is luck indeed! Coincidence seldom comes so pat. You're the very man I wanted to see. I've made my first appearance on this or any other stage as an art-patron to-day, and I'd like you to come and judge of my purchase. What do you say to this, now?' And he held up the water-colour, which lay beside him still on the rustic seat, for Mansel's critical and professional opinion.

The artist glanced at it with a smile of recognition.

'What, Linnell's?' he cried. 'Oh, I saw it earlier. I've watched it along through all its stages. It's a very good sketch—very good indeed. He never did better to my mind, with an English subject. Not over-elaborated with those finikin touches which often spoil Linnell's best work. It's a perfect little idyll in green and ultramarine.' And he eyed it appreciatively.

'You like it, then?' Dumaresq asked in a curious tone.

'Like it? Well, of course. One can't help liking everything of Linnell's. He has the true touch of genius in all his work, if only he were a little bit less supremely self-conscious.'

'What do you think I gave for it?' the old man suggested, with his head on one side like a critical connoisseur.

'Gave for it?' Mansel repeated with an incredulous stare. 'You don't mean to say, then, Dumaresq, you've actually bought it?'

'Bought it and paid for it,' the philosopher answered, with something very like unphilosophic complacency, enjoying his hearer's obvious surprise. 'Ah, you didn't think I went in for pictures! Well, I don't, as a rule: I leave those things to the great of this world. But, you see, as this was a special subject, of peculiar interest to myself and Psyche, I thought I couldn't let it fall to a mere stranger. I'd fix it at once: I'd keep it in the family. So I commissioned it beforehand, I think you call it; and when Linnell came round this afternoon I paid him his price and gi'ed it in hond, like the Northern Farmer. How much should you say, now, I ought to have spent upon it?'

Mansel regarded first the picture and then the philosopher in hesitating silence for a few seconds.

'Well,' he said irresolutely, after an awkward pause, 'I don't know, of course, what Linnell's likely to have put it at for you; no doubt he let you have it a little cheaper; but the picture as a picture is worth fifty guineas.'

'Fifty guineas!' Dumaresq echoed in dismayed astonishment.

'Yes, fifty guineas,' Mansel answered quietly. 'Linnell commands his market, you know. He could get that for it any day in London.'

Haviland Dumaresq's gray eyes flashed sudden fire. His first thought was that Linnell had been guilty of rank disrespect to his person and position in letting him have a fifty-guinea picture at considerably less than half-price. Poor he might be—he had sat up half last night, indeed, toiling like a galley-slave at a penny-a-lining article on the Conservation of Energy for his hard task-masters' 'Popular Instructor' at eight shillings a page—but what right had a painter fellow whom he'd hardly even seen in his life yet, to lower prices for *him*, like a beggarly skinflint, or to take it for granted he couldn't with ease, from the plenitude of his wealth, spare fifty guineas?

His second thought was that a man who could earn fifty guineas 'any day in London' for a bit of a water-colour no bigger than a page of the *Athenæum*, might perhaps after all be able to make Psyche happy.

'That's a very large sum,' he said, drawing a long breath and looking hard at Mansel. 'Men of letters get nothing like that for their work, I'm afraid. But, then, they don't have anything to sell which can minister to the selfish monopolist vanity of the rich and idle. No Manchester merchant can hang upon his walls a unique copy of "Paradise Lost" or a solitary exemplar of the "Novum Organum," and say to his friends after dinner with vulgar pride: "Look here, So-and-so, that's Milton's or Bacon's greatest work. I paid fifty thousand guineas down for that lot." Still, even so, I'm surprised to hear you painters earn your money so easily. Twenty guineas seemed to me in my ignorance a very big price indeed to pay for it.'

'Oh, Linnell can get that readily enough,'

Mansel answered with a short uneasy laugh. 'His oils he sells at good prices at Christie's. His water colours are snapped up every year at the Institute. But then, you know, they take him a good bit of time. He's a slow worker, and doesn't get through many canvases in the course of a twelvemonth.'

'Now, how much do you suppose a painter of his sort ought to earn on an average per annum?' Dumaresq asked offhand, with too evident an assumption of easy carelessness. 'How would his income compare, for example, with an author's or a journalist's?'

'Well, I really can't say,' Mansel answered, smiling, and perceiving his questioner's drift at once. 'Perhaps some five or six hundred, all told; perhaps a thousand; perhaps more than that. But then,' he added, his thoughts keeping pace all along with Dumaresq's, 'he may have private means of his own as well, you know. He spends freely. I've never known him pressed for cash. I don't think he lives altogether on his pictures.'

' No ?'—with keen interest.

'No; I should say not. I've always imagined he had means of his own. For one thing, he had plenty, I know, at Christ Church.'

'He was at Christ Church, was he?' Dumaresq put in reflectively. 'An expensive college—the most fashionable at Oxford. A man must have money who goes to Christ Church!'

'Not necessarily,' Mansel answered, putting him off the scent once more. 'I was there myself, you remember, and Heaven knows I was poor enough in those days, in all conscience. But then, I had a studentship of eighty pounds a year, which makes a difference, of course: whereas Linnell came up as an ordinary commoner.'

'And you think he has money, then?' Dumaresq asked eagerly.

'I think so. But, mind, I know nothing about it. Linnell was always the most reticent and mysterious of men, full of small reserves and petty mystifications. He never told anybody a word about himself. He's always been close, provokingly close. For aught I know, he may be as poor as a church mouse in reality; and for aught I know, again, he may be as rich as Crœsus. So far as my observation goes, he always acts like a wealthy man, and talks like a poor one. But if anybody ever taxes him with opulence, he resents the imputation as a positive slight, and declares with effusion he's almost on the very verge of beggary.'

'Many rich men,' Dumaresq mused dreamily, 'are pursued with a peculiar form of mania called *timor paupertatis*, and what you say's just one of its recognised symptoms—that the sufferer never will admit his wealth, for fear other people should try to swindle him or rob him or beg of him. You may remember that in the fourth volume of the " Encyclopædic Philosophy"—the volume that deals with Heteropathic Affections in the Empirical Individual—I bring the phenomenon of concealment of wealth under the same law with the pseudomorphic corrugation of cooling nebulæ and the facts of mimicry in animal evolution. It's a most interesting branch of psychological study. I shall watch this young man. I shall watch him—I shall watch him.'

He spoke in a droning, half-sleepy undertone; and Mansel, who had seen the great thinker more than once in this state before, and who always felt creepy at the strange look in his eyes, made haste to concoct some plausible excuse for a hurried departure.

'When Dumaresq gets into that curious vein,' he said to himself internally, 'philosopher or no philosopher, he's simply unendurable. From a man of singular intellect and genius, he dwindles down at once into a mere bore. All his brilliancy and ability seems to desert him, and he talks platitudes to you three times over in varying language, like the veriest old driveller at the Seniors in London. When these fits come upon him, the wise man will do well to leave him alone. He goes silly for the nonce: *hunc tu Romane caveto.*' And he walked off, whistling, to his own studio.

But Haviland Dumaresq, having learned all he wanted from Linnell's friend, strolled away by himself, regardless of lunch, upon the open Downs, that overlook the sea with their bare green knolls and their deep curved hollows. He strolled along, crushing rich flowers under foot as he went, wrapped up in his own thoughts, and with the poison within him gaining deeper and deeper hold upon his swimming and reeling brain each moment. The sun shone high over the purple sea; the hills rolled boundless and undulating before him; the noise of the bell upon the foremost wether of the ruddled flock that cropped close grass in the combe hard by rang distant in his ear like most delicious music. Birds sang; bees hummed; gorse crackled; grasshoppers chirped; the scent of wild thyme hung thick on the air. The opium was transforming earth into heaven for him. Space swelled, as it always swelled into infinite abysses for Haviland Dumaresq when the intoxicating drug had once taken full possession of his veins and fibres. The horizon spread boundless in vast perspective with its clear blue line against the pale gray sky; the shadows in the hollow combes lengthened and deepened into romantic gloom; the hills rose up in huge expansive throes, and became as high mountains to his dilated vision. A white gull flapped its gleaming wings overhead : to Dumaresq it revealed itself as some monstrous albatross. His own stature even seemed to double itself as he stalked along the dividing line of open ridge, till he loomed in his own eyes larger than human on the bald and rounded crest of the gigantic hog's back. All nature assumed a more heroic cast : he walked no longer our prosaic world : each step appeared to carry him over illimitable space : he trod with Dante the broad floor of Paradise.

And wonderful vistas opened ahead for Psyche also. She, too, his darling, she, too, should be happy. This man who had come to woo her in disguise, he was rich, he was great, there was mystery about him. In his present ecstatic frame of mind, Haviland Dumaresq hugged and magnified the mystery. The poetic element in his nature, sternly repressed by the philosophic side in his saner moments, found free vent at times in the unnatural exaltation of narcotic excitement, and ran riot in wild day-dreams of impossible splendour. He had passed through the golden gate to-day. He saw his Psyche decked out in all the barbaric splendour of pearl and diamond that his soul despised : he saw her floating in silks and gauzy stuffs and laces : he saw her circling round in the giddy dance, one blaze of glory, in the glittering rooms and slippery halls that he hated and eschewed as surviving relics of savage and barbaric anti-social luxury. High-stepping grays whirled her along in state in a light and graceful carriage through thronged thoroughfares of over-wealthy fashion. Flunkeys, whom Haviland Dumaresq could have kicked with pleasure, bowed, door in servile hand, to see her take her seat on the padded cushions. Massive silver and Venetian glass and hideous marvels of cunning architecture in ice and sugar loaded the table at whose head she sat in dainty brocade or in shimmering satin. Money, money, money, money: the dross he despised, the pleasure he looked down upon, the vulgar aims and ends he himself had cast like dirt behind him —he dreamed them all for the daughter he loved, and was no longer ashamed: for Haviland Dumaresq the philosopher was dead within him now, and there remained for the moment but that shell or husk, Haviland Dumaresq the incipient opium-eater. He had forgotten everything but the joy of his day-dream, and he stalked ever forward, more asleep than awake, yet walking on sturdily, with exalted nerves, towards the edge of the Down, to the broad blue sea, that danced and gleamed with pearl and sapphire in the bright sunshine before him.

CHAPTER XII.

THE BUBBLE BURSTS.

SUDDENLY, after walking on in a dreamy way for miles and miles over the springy turf, he hardly knew how, the old man found himself beside a clump of gorse, face to face with the mysterious painter fellow. He started at the sight. Linnell had come up to the Downs, too, to walk off his chagrin, and to swallow as best he might his disappointment at not seeing Psyche.

Always sensitive, the young artist was more morbidly sensitive than usual where women were concerned. To say the truth, he had known but little of woman's society. Rich as he was and cultivated to the finger-ends, the circumstances of his life had thrown Linnell to an exceptionally small degree into contact with families. His world was a world of clubs and studios and men's lounging-places: so little had he seen of the other sex that he hardly felt himself at home, even now in a lady's drawing-room.

This was not to be wondered at. His mother had died before he left America; at Oxford he had fallen in with none but college acquaintances; his English cousins refused to acknowledge him: and the Boston-bred lad, shy and ill at ease from his congenital lameness, and the strangeness of the novel surroundings in whose midst he was thrown, found himself cast at nineteen entirely on his own resources in the matter of gaining an introduction into our cold and austere English Society. It wasn't surprising, therefore, that he knew hardly anyone except his brother-painters ; or that he loved to escape from the vast blank of London life to the freedom and the space of the African desert. There at least he felt perfectly at home with the world : there no Bedouin ever trod on his social corns, no distracting matron ever strove to win him from his Bohemian solitude to the irksome respectability of white ties or five o'clock tea-tables.

So Linnell, perhaps, made a little more of a girl's fancy, as he thought it, than most other men of his age and position would have dreamed of doing. He had retired to the Downs to brood over the supposed slight to his feelings in private ; but a brisk walk upon the bracing turf, all alive with orchids and blue viper's bugloss, had almost succeeded in restoring him to equanimity again, when all at once a sudden turn into a small combe brought him up sharp, with unexpected abruptness, full in front of Haviland Dumaresq.

The old man gazed at him vacantly for a moment. His eyes were glazed and very hazy; they explored space for some seconds with a distant interest. Then, on a sudden, he seemed to wake up into life with a start, and recognising the painter with a burst of intuition, laid his hand with quite a kindly air upon Linnell's shoulder.

The gesture took the young man completely by surprise, for Dumaresq was one of those self-restrained, self-respecting natures whose strong sense of individuality in others assumes the form of an almost instinctive shrinking from anything that borders upon personal contact. Linnell looked the philosopher back in the face with a melting expression of mingled doubt and pleasure, as he hesitated slightly.

'I wanted to speak with you, Linnell,' Haviland Dumaresq began in a dreamy voice, motioning the young man over to a dry bank in the broad sunshine. 'I want, in point of fact, to apologize, or at least to explain to you. I'm afraid I was perhaps a trifle brusque with you at my cottage this morning. No, don't say I wasn't; I know I spoke sharply. Perhaps I even hurt your feelings. My training in life has not, I fear, been of a sort to encourage sensitiveness in myself, or to make me sympathize with it as much as I ought in others. I'm aware that I often err in that respect. But if I erred it was not through any personal intent, but under the influence of a strong impelling motive. I've been exercised in mind a good deal of late. There's something, in short, I want to speak about to you.'

He went on still in a thick, half-dreamy, wandering tone, and his dilated pupils seemed to fix themselves vaguely on a point in infinity; but he delivered his words with regularity and ease, though somewhat stiffly, and it was evident to Linnell that he was making a very strong effort to master himself for some great object, under the influence of some fierce overpowering emotion. The painter allowed the old man to lead him unresisting to the bank, and took his seat beside him with a beating heart, wondering what of good or evil for himself or Psyche this strange exordium might prove to forebode, and anxiously awaiting its further development.

'I wasn't at all annoyed, Mr. Dumaresq,' he said in a low voice, perhaps not quite truthfully; 'only a little grieved that a man —well— whom I so much admired and respected as yourself, should refuse to accept so small a present from me.'

'But it cost you a good deal of time and trouble,' Dumaresq answered slowly, in the same fixed, mechanical, far-away voice; 'and time is money, you know, Linnell—time is money. I shouldn't feel it right to occupy so much of a young man's time without making him what I thought an adequate repayment. You must forgive me that: it's a principle of mine: rather a sacrifice to my own ideas as to individuality than an act of unfriendliness toward any particular person.' Then he added suddenly in a very different tone: 'I'm an old man, you must remember—a worn-out old man. I've wasted my life in a hard service—the service of science, the service of humanity. Bear with me, bear with me, a little while, I beg of you. I'm an old, old man. There's not much now left of me.'

Linnell was touched by his appealing look—the look for a moment of the real Haviland Dumaresq, who felt in his great heart the full pathos of his own unrequited sacrifice for the good of his kind, as he firmly believed it.

'Indeed,' the young man made answer

earnestly, 'I wasn't vexed, Mr. Dumaresq. I only wanted you to accept a small tribute, in part payment, as a single instalment, from one who owes to you intellectually and morally more than he can ever find words to tell you. And as to the picture, it really didn't take me long. I value my own work very lightly indeed. I should have thought myself more than repaid for my pains in painting it if a man whom I respect and revere so much would have condescended to accept it from me and keep it as a memento.'

'You remember what I told you the other evening,' the old man replied, with a more searching glance at his companion's features. 'Do as I say, my friend, and not as I do, if you wish to flourish. Don't despise money foolishly—as I have done. My advice to a young man setting out in life is simply this: Follow the world; the world is wisest. You can't afford to fling away sovereigns like water. You're a painter, and you must live by the practice of your art. Now, why did you sell me that picture so cheap? Mansel came in after you'd left this morning, and told me you could have got fifty guineas for it any day in London.' He clasped his hand gently round the painter's arm. 'Don't be utopian, my dear fellow,' he went on with unwonted colloquialism. 'Tell me why you let me have it for twenty.'

Linnell blushed and hesitated a moment. At last he determined to blurt out the truth and shame the devil. 'Because I knew you couldn't afford more, Mr. Dumaresq,' he said shyly.

Haviland Dumaresq did not resent the unexpected remark. 'You were right,' he answered with a sigh. 'I am poor, poor. The money I gave you was all I had in the house just then. You have been quite frank with me, and I'm quite frank with you in return. I have still to earn to-morrow's dinner.'

A strange doubt flitted for a moment across Linnell's mind. His eight hundred guineas, then? What on earth could have become of them? Was it possible that Haviland Dumaresq, the deepest and broadest of living thinkers, could stoop to tell him so despicable a lie? But no! impossible! He rejected the idea with scorn, as any man with one spark of nobility in his nature must needs have rejected it. No doubt Macmurdo and White hadn't yet sent in their annual account. The secret of Dumaresq's new-made opulence was not yet out; he was still unaware of the magnificent sum of which he was already potentially master.

'It's terrible,' the young man said, breaking the short pause, 'that after all you have wrought and done for the world you should still be able to say *that* to-day—

you, the greatest thinker in our modern Europe.'

'Not for me,' the old stoic answered with a resigned nod : 'not terrible for me : I'm used to it : it suits me ; but for Psyche, I grant you, yes : for Psyche ; for Psyche.'

'Miss Dumaresq deserves all the world can give her,' Linnell replied boldly.

The old man's eye fired up once more with a brilliant flash, and then grew slowly dim again. If only he could see his way to make Psyche happy ! He wasn't sordidly anxious to sell her for gold : oh no, oh no ; he would sell her to no man : but he wanted to see his Psyche happy. He clutched Linnell's hand once more and spoke earnestly, fervently. 'Listen here,' he cried in more vivid tones ; 'you're a friend—a disciple. I can tell you. I can trust you. I know I've thrown away my own life : I could endure that easily, if that were all ; but that's not all. I've thrown away hers too; I've failed in my duty to her. You can't think how that wrong weighs upon my spirit now. I ought to have toiled and moiled and slaved and sweated, not to write the "Encyclopædic Philosophy" for the good of the race—how little that matters!—but to carve out for my child a place in the world well worthy of her. One or the other course I might rightly have pursued; but not both together. If I meant to devote my life to philosophy, I should never have been a father. Becoming a father, I ought to have devoted my life to *her* alone. I gave a hostage to fortune, and I failed to redeem it. I became responsible for a life, and I failed to guarantee it a proper future. And now in my helpless old age I see my error. I see it too late; I see it too late; I see it, and I pay for it.'

'You are wrong,' Linnell answered firmly. 'So great a life as yours demands a great account to be given at last of it. The vast organizing genius, the wonderful brain that conceived and wrought out the " Encyclopædic Philosophy," was not only your own to do as you would with: it was a gift held in trust by you for the world and for the ages. You played your part well. It is for us, the remainder, who profit by your just and due yet none the less splendid and self-sacrificing use of your own great powers, to see that neither you nor she is a loser by your grand and unselfish action.'

'You think so?' the old man asked, looking up at him with a passing expression of doubt.

Linnell hesitated, like one caught in a trap. Was the philosopher trying to probe his secret? 'I think so,' he answered aloud after a short struggle.

'Then that brings me back at once to what I wanted to say to you in confidence to-day,'

Dumaresq continued, glancing at him with a strangely remorseful face. 'Mr. Linnell, I'm going to trust you. You understand exactly how I feel towards Psyche. I know how sweet and rare a flower it is that blooms around the wreck of my ruined life. I know it, and I cherish her as she ought to be cherished—jealously, scrupulously, reverently, tenderly. I want my child to fill her proper place in life: I want to see her happy before I die. Unless she goes away to fill it and to be happy—well, I hope she may cling to the ruin still while there's anything left of it to hold together.'

'Yes,' Linnell answered, half chilled by his words. He sympathized, in a way, with that strange old man; but Dumaresq had struck by accident the feeblest of all the resonant chords in his complex nature for a father to work upon. No apt response could there be expected.

'Yes,' the old man answered, his eyes growing tenderer each moment as he spoke, and his lips quivering. 'Pardon me if I've noticed your feelings towards my daughter. I know you've been seeing a great deal of Psyche lately. I know Psyche's been thinking a great deal of you. It surprises you that I should have noticed it! Ah, well, that shows you don't know how closely I watch over Psyche. You fancy I'm blind to these things, because I'm old, and a dreamer, and a philosopher, and a stoic. No doubt, where human trivialities are concerned, I'm often blind; I see nothing. You can't keep your whole soul fixed at once upon the main order of the cosmos and the minutest details of Mrs. Grundy's dinner-parties. But where even the veriest trivialities touch my Psyche, my eyes are at once as sharp as a lynx's. Then the blind bat wakes up and sees: the mole opens his narrow eyelids, shakes the dust of grimy burrowings from his coat, creeps out from his hole, and peers about him with the sharp vision of a very Argus. That's how it is when Psyche's in question.' He took Linnell's hand in his own for a moment once more. 'Bear with me,' he went on pleadingly —'bear with a father who asks you only because he loves his daughter. I don't want to see her affections too deeply engaged without knowing what are the prospects of her future happiness. You love Psyche; oh yes, I know it. You can't conceal *that* from me. I have eyes. I see it. But before Psyche commits herself to loving *you*, I must earnestly ask you—as a father, I feel compelled to ask you—are you in a position to marry?—have you the means and the power to make Psyche happy?'

It was not an unnatural question for a father to put, as fathers go: even a man less hardly tried by fortune and less devoted to his daughter than Haviland Dumaresq might easily have asked it. But nothing could have been worse adapted for meeting a man of Linnell's nature. The painter's quick suspicion was aroused at once. Dumaresq's ardour chilled him.

'I never said,' he answered, disengaging his hand with difficulty from the old man's grasp, 'that I made any pretensions to be regarded as one of Miss Dumaresq's suitors. That honour is one I never ventured to claim. It would be the more usual course to ask me such a question as you now ask me when I came before you of my own accord to beg your consent, after I had already made sure of your daughter's wishes. As it is, you discount the future somewhat too brusquely— you have no reason to suppose my feelings towards Miss Dumaresq are anything warmer than those of the merest polite admiration.'

'The more usual course!' Haviland Dumaresq answered, looking across at him with a profoundly surprised air. 'The more usual course! and Psyche's happiness at stake! Ah, Linnell, Linnell, you don't know how I watch over her! Where Psyche's concerned, do you think it matters to me one farthing what's usual? I know how you feel. You're young, and you love her. For you, and for her, that would be quite enough, of course. At your ages, that's all young blood should think about. In the fitness of things, I acknowledge your attitude. But *me!* I tell you, it's my duty to guard her with all my soul from her own too hasty or too foolish feelings. I know what it all means—poverty; long waiting; a cheek grown pale with hope deferred; an imprudent marriage at last; my darling worn out with infinite petty cares and sordid shifts of a young family, brought up too scantily. I've seen it and known it.

Would it be right of me to let Psyche expose herself to all that? If I see you're beginning to think of my Psyche, mustn't I make sure for myself beforehand who and what you are, and what you can do to make her happy? Don't suppose I'm so blind as not to know you think of her. No man reads emotional expression worse than I do, I know—my mind moves on a different plane from that—but I must be a poor reader and speller indeed if I couldn't spell out what's written in letters as big as my fist across your very forehead— what pervades every act and look and word of yours whenever I see you one moment near her. So I venture to ask you now in plain words beforehand, if my Psyche loves you as you love her, are you in a position to make her happy?'

'Mr. Dumaresq,' Linnell cried, taken aback, 'I beg of you, I pray you, whatever you do, not to breathe or whisper one word of this to—to Psyche. I can't bear to think that Haviland Dumaresq should be capable of speaking to me in such a strain; for many reasons which you will readily guess, it would surprise and distress your daughter even more profoundly. Don't let her know—pure, and beautiful, and shrinking as she is—don't let her know you have so thrust her name in such a connection upon a perfect stranger. For her sake, for the sake of her maidenly dignity, which *I* at least respect if *you* do not, forbear to speak to me any more about her. I will not admit I have any other feeling on earth towards Miss Dumaresq; but I have at least too much reverence and regard for her position to breathe her name to any man living before I have asked her own permission to discuss her.'

Haviland Dumaresq paused irresolute for a moment; then he answered once more, in a very soft voice:

'You say well,' he murmured; 'but— you admit the impeachment. What you allow is more than what you deny. I won't put my question, therefore, on the ground to which you object; but I will ask you plainly, as a matter of general abstract information, which I'm anxious to obtain, have you any means of your own of a private sort, or do you live—well, entirely by the practice of your profession?'

'And I will answer you,' Linnell replied, drawing himself up with a determined air, 'that the question of my income is one which lies entirely between myself and the Commissioners of Inland Revenue.'

'Your answer is evasive,' Dumaresq said, drawing back and eyeing him hard with that keen clear glance of his. 'If anything except Psyche's happiness were at stake, I ought to take the hint and forbear to press you. But *there* I can't help myself: for the very way in which you say it makes me see you're trying to hide from me, for some inexplicable reason, the fact that you have money.' He drew his hand across his forehead with a vague dim air. Again the strange dreaminess seemed to come like a cloud across him. His eye grew glazed. 'For myself,' he went on slowly, 'I care nothing for money. You know I care nothing. For myself I despise it. Have I not worked like a galley-slave all my life long, on bread and water sometimes, in the service of truth, caring for nothing— money, honour, fame—if only I could fulfil my appointed life-task? When did any man bribe me with gold or with position? When did any man turn me from my high purpose? But for Psyche, oh, for Psyche, I'm very jealous. I can't bear to think that Psyche should lead a life of drudgery. I toil hard for her now; but I can't toil much longer. I'm almost worn out. I want to know that after my time Psyche will be happy. It would be wrong for me to let her get her affections engaged with anyone who hasn't the means to keep her as she deserves to be kept. That must be my excuse for reading your secret. At any rate, I've read it. I can see it—I can see it: I can see you have money.' He repeated the word dreamily once or twice to himself, 'Money, money, money, money.'

Linnell recoiled from him with a startled look of surprise and annoyance. Had he known under what strange influence Haviland Dumaresq spoke, he might have been less astonished: as it was, he could hardly believe these words came from the lips of the Encyclopædic Philosopher and Psyche's father! The painter's disillusionment was indeed for the moment complete. His idol had truly feet of clay.

'You make a mistake,' he answered coldly,

with a repellent air. 'But I myself am in no way answerable for it. I have never given either you or Miss Dumaresq the slightest reason for believing that I laid any claim in any way to the possession of riches. If the thought ever occurred to me—and I do not say it did—that I might perhaps venture to aspire—that I might ask Miss Dumaresq to share her life with me, then certainly it occurred to me only in the form that I might ask her to share a journeyman painter's early struggles —and perhaps in the end his success also. I thought she would sympathize with such an attitude. I thought she would not refuse to aid me in my first endeavours. If I asked at all, I would ask Miss Dumaresq to accept me just as I am; to take me for the sake of myself and my art; to inspire my work and to accept my devotion. It surprises me to hear you talk as you do.' He paused for a moment. 'If I had not heard it from your own lips,' he added slowly, 'I could never have believed it of Haviland Dumaresq. Even now, I cannot believe but that Haviland Dumaresq's daughter would surely behave in a way more befitting her father's character. If ever she marries any man, she will marry him, I firmly hold, not for money, not for position, not even for happiness, but just because she loves him. And if ever I asked Miss Dumaresq to accept me, it would be on that ground, and on that ground alone, that I could think of asking her.'

Were ever unconformable natures more inopportunely thrown together? By pure accident, either's angles offended the other mortally. They came so close in most ways, yet with such unfortunate capacities for creating mutual misunderstandings.

The old man's face relaxed rapidly. The collapse from an opium paradise is often almost miraculous in its suddenness. The gay bubble bursts even more quickly and strangely than it swelled. As Haviland Dumaresq sat and listened to Linnell's cold and guarded answer, the effect of the drug, which was already beginning naturally to wear off under the influence of exercise, cleared away all at once in a horrid awakening, when the disenchanted dreamer recognised at a single stroke his own needless degradation, and the total downfall of the magnificent palace he had been rearing for an hour or two on such an airy basis. In a second the illusion was utterly dispelled. Space shrank once more like an empty bladder to its normal dimensions. The mountains fell slowly into long flat Downs. The colour faded from earth and sky. The sea subsided to its natural level. The perspective of the world restored itself at once in all its ordinary meanness. And Linnell the mysterious stood revealed before him after all as a mere hard-working, penniless, struggling painter, with nothing but the chances of his art to subsist upon. Not such the dream he had cherished for Psyche. She must marry someone who could keep her at least in modest luxury—or else cling to the ruin.

'Then — you — have — no — means?' he gasped out slowly, clutching the stem of the elder-bush at his side for support, and gazing hard into the painter's face.

'Miss Dumaresq would not ask for money,' Linnell replied with an evasive smile.

The old man's face fell slowly.

'Have you nearly finished your picture?' he asked at last in a very quiet voice.

With a start of unwelcome surprise, Linnell divined his meaning at once. But he repressed his feelings.

'Another day will finish it,' he answered in the self-same unemotional tone, as coldly as the philosopher himself had spoken.

'That is well. Come to-morrow and get it finished,' Haviland Dumaresq said with reluctant determination.

Linnell bowed.

'And after that?' he asked, looking hard into the old man's face.

'And after that,' Dumaresq answered, leaning forward apologetically, 'I think, for Psyche's sake, for all our sakes—it would be better she and you should not meet again. Ah yes, I pain you! You fancy I'm hard. You fancy I'm cruel. That's just because I'm really so tender. I feel it my duty to guard my daughter from the bare chance of misery, poverty, drudgery. Drudgery! I know what it means, my friend. For a man, those things are easy enough to bear; but for a woman—tenderly, delicately nurtured—how could I expose her to them? I must not; I cannot. I've gained experience myself on my path through life. I paid for it dear. Psyche shall have the benefit of it for nothing. No penniless man shall drag her down, down, down, to a wretched struggle with sordid poverty. Psyche is beautiful ; Psyche is intelligent ; Psyche is animated ; Psyche is clever. She has been much admired. She's reaching the age when a girl should come out. If I take her to London—and I'd work my fingers to the bone to do it—she can mix in society and meet the sort of man she ought to meet with. I may be poor, but I'm not unknown. My name is worth much. I can get introductions, invitations, acquaintances for Psyche. Once seen in London, she's sure to marry, and to marry as she ought. I must guard her for the present from throwing away her life for a future of drudgery.'

'I see,' Linnell answered bitterly. 'You think the world's wisdom for women is summed up in that one short phrase—to marry well—do you ?'

'You say it yourself,' Dumaresq answered oracularly. '*You* say it, not *I*. But perhaps you're right, after all. To marry well! It means what the wisdom of the world has made it mean—to marry where the means of happiness are best forthcoming.' He said it musingly.

Linnell bowed his head once more in solemn acquiescence. 'I may see Miss Dumaresq to-morrow?' he asked after a pause.

'You may come in and finish your picture, of course. That's mere common justice. Take as many days as you find needful to finish it. I wouldn't waste so much valuable work for worlds by curtailing in any way your opportunities for completing it.'

'And I may see her *alone?*' the painter asked again, trembling.

Dumaresq hesitated. 'Yes, you may see her alone,' he answered after a moment's consideration; 'but you know my views, and as a man of honour, you will not try to take advantage, I'm sure, of the permission—I may even say the concession I make to you. You will not incite a girl of seventeen to differ from her own father on an important matter affecting her future. I allow you to see her only because it's possible you may have already said things to her you would now wish to withdraw or to explain away. I rely upon your sense of honour for the rest.' He faltered for a moment with a sudden servile air. 'I'm an old man,' he repeated once more, almost humbly; 'I only want to make Psyche happy.'

The last two sentences were plaintively said. They touched Linnell somehow, in spite of himself.

'Very well,' he replied; 'you may rely upon me, then.' He looked at Dumaresq fixedly. 'I have come to the age of disillusionments,' he went on; 'but no disillusion I've ever had in all my life was half so bitter as this of to-day has been. I have seen with my own eyes a king of men dethroned from his high seat—a prince of thinkers lowered from his pinnacle to the level of the commonest and vulgarest humanity. But for the sake of what you have said, I will spare you more. Miss Dumaresq shall never marry a penniless painter.'

'Oh, remember, it's for her sake,' the old man cried appealingly, wringing his hands, and now unstrung by the sudden collapse of the opium-ecstasy. 'It's for *her* sake, remember! Don't be too hard upon me, I beseech you, Linnell. She's very young: I must guard her youth, her ignorance, her innocence. I should be doing wrong as a father if I didn't preserve her from the fatal consequences of her own impetuousness, as we take away knives from very young children. It's my duty to guide her by my elder experience. Many a woman who married herself for love at twenty—and led a life of hopeless drudgery—regrets it enough when she's reached fifty to make her daughters marry better than she did. The world knows best: the world knows best: it is wiser by far than any one of its component members.'

'Good-bye,' Linnell answered, rising up with an effort from the dreary bank. 'I'll call in to finish the picture at ten to-morrow.'

'At ten to-morrow!' Haviland Dumaresq repeated in a dreamy voice. 'At ten to-morrow! Good-bye for the present, then. It's for Psyche's sake. At ten to-morrow.'

And sinking down on the bank, when Linnell was gone, he buried his face in his hands like a child and sobbed bitterly. 'I hope I've done right,' he cried to himself in his profound despair; 'I hope I've done right. Perhaps I'm wrong. But I never could sell my Psyche to a life of drudgery!'

END OF VOL. I.

BILLING AND SONS, PRINTERS, GUILDFORD.

June, 1891.

A List of Books
PUBLISHED BY
CHATTO & WINDUS,
214, Piccadilly, London, W.

Sold by all Booksellers, or sent post-free for the published price by the Publishers.

ABOUT.—THE FELLAH: An Egyptian Novel. By EDMOND ABOUT. Translated by Sir RANDAL ROBERTS. Post 8vo, illustrated boards, 2s.

ADAMS (W. DAVENPORT), WORKS BY.
A DICTIONARY OF THE DRAMA. Being a comprehensive Guide to the Plays, Playwrights, Players, and Playhouses of the United Kingdom and America. Crown 8vo, half-bound, 12s. 6d. [*Preparing.*
QUIPS AND QUIDDITIES. Selected by W. D. ADAMS. Post 8vo, cloth limp, 2s. 6d.

ADAMS (W. H. D.).—WITCH, WARLOCK, AND MAGICIAN: Historical Sketches of Magic and Witchcraft in England and Scotland. By W. H. DAVENPORT ADAMS. Demy 8vo, cloth extra, 12s.

AGONY COLUMN (THE) OF "THE TIMES," from 1800 to 1870. Edited, with an Introduction, by ALICE CLAY. Post 8vo, cloth limp, 2s. 6d.

AIDE (HAMILTON), WORKS BY. Post 8vo, illustrated boards, 2s. each.
CARR OF CARRLYON. | CONFIDENCES.

ALBERT.—BROOKE FINCHLEY'S DAUGHTER. By MARY ALBERT. Post 8vo, picture boards, 2s.; cloth limp, 2s. 6d.

ALEXANDER (MRS.), NOVELS BY. Post 8vo, illustrated boards, 2s. each.
MAID, WIFE, OR WIDOW? | VALERIE'S FATE.

ALLEN (GRANT), WORKS BY. Crown 8vo, cloth extra, 6s. each.
THE EVOLUTIONIST AT LARGE. | COLIN CLOUT'S CALENDAR.
VIGNETTES FROM NATURE.

Crown 8vo, cloth extra, 6s. each; post 8vo, illustrated boards., 2s. each
STRANGE STORIES. With a Frontispiece by GEORGE DU MAURIER.
THE BECKONING HAND. With a Frontispiece by TOWNLEY GREEN.

Crown 8vo, cloth extra, 3s. 6d. each; post 8vo, illustrated boards, 2s. each.
PHILISTIA. | FOR MAIMIE'S SAKE. | THIS MORTAL COIL.
BABYLON. | IN ALL SHADES. | THE TENTS OF SHEM.
| THE DEVIL'S DIE. |

THE GREAT TABOO. Crown 8vo, cloth extra, 3s. 6d.
DUMARESQ'S DAUGHTER. Three Vols., crown 8vo. [*Shortly.*

AMERICAN LITERATURE, A LIBRARY OF, from the Earliest Settlement to the Present Time. Compiled and Edited by EDMUND CLARENCE STEDMAN and ELLEN MACKAY HUTCHINSON. Eleven Vols., royal 8vo, cloth extra. A few copies are for sale by Messrs. CHATTO & WINDUS (published in New York by C. L. WEBSTER & Co.), price £6 12s. the set.

ARCHITECTURAL STYLES, A HANDBOOK OF. By A. ROSENGARTEN. Translated by W. COLLETT-SANDARS. With 639 Illusts. Cr. 8vo, cl. ex., 7s. 6d.

ART (THE) OF AMUSING: A Collection of Graceful Arts, Games, Tricks, Puzzles, and Charades. By FRANK BELLEW. 300 Illusts. Cr. 8vo, cl. ex., 4s. 6d.

BOOKS PUBLISHED BY

ARNOLD (EDWIN LESTER), WORKS BY.
THE WONDERFUL ADVENTURES OF PHRA THE PHŒNICIAN. With Introduction by Sir EDWIN ARNOLD, and 12 Illusts. by H. M. PAGET. Cr. 8vo, cl., 3s. 6d.
BIRD LIFE IN ENGLAND. Crown 8vo, cloth extra, 6s.

ARTEMUS WARD'S WORKS: The Works of CHARLES FARRER BROWNE, better known as ARTEMUS WARD. With Portrait and Facsimile. Crown 8vo, cloth extra, 7s. 6d.—Also a POPULAR EDITION, post 8vo, picture boards, 2s.
THE GENIAL SHOWMAN: Life and Adventures of ARTEMUS WARD. By EDWARD P. HINGSTON. With a Frontispiece. Crown 8vo, cloth extra 3s. 6d.

ASHTON (JOHN), WORKS BY. Crown 8vo, cloth extra, 7s. 6d. each.
HISTORY OF THE CHAP-BOOKS OF THE 18th CENTURY. With 334 Illusts.
SOCIAL LIFE IN THE REIGN OF QUEEN ANNE. With 85 Illustrations.
HUMOUR, WIT, AND SATIRE OF SEVENTEENTH CENTURY. With 82 Illusts.
ENGLISH CARICATURE AND SATIRE ON NAPOLEON THE FIRST. 115 Illusts.
MODERN STREET BALLADS. With 57 Illustrations.

BACTERIA.—A SYNOPSIS OF THE BACTERIA AND YEAST FUNGI AND ALLIED SPECIES. By W. B. GROVE, B.A. With 87 Illustrations. Crown 8vo, cloth extra, 3s. 6d.

BARDSLEY (REV. C. W.), WORKS BY.
ENGLISH SURNAMES: Their Sources and Significations. Cr. 8vo, cloth, 7s. 6d.
CURIOSITIES OF PURITAN NOMENCLATURE. Crown 8vo, cloth extra, 6s.

BARING GOULD (S., Author of "John Herring," &c.), NOVELS BY. Crown 8vo, cloth extra, 3s. 6d. each; post 8vo, illustrated boards, 2s. each.
RED SPIDER. | EVE.

BARRETT (FRANK, Author of "Lady Biddy Fane,") NOVELS BY. Post 8vo, illustrated boards, 2s. each; cloth, 2s. 6d. each.
FETTERED FOR LIFE. | BETWEEN LIFE AND DEATH.

BEACONSFIELD, LORD: A Biography. By T. P. O'CONNOR, M P. Sixth Edition, with an Introduction. Crown 8vo, cloth extra, 5s.

BEAUCHAMP.—GRANTLEY GRANGE: A Novel. By SHELSLEY BEAUCHAMP. Post 8vo, illustrated boards, 2s.

BEAUTIFUL PICTURES BY BRITISH ARTISTS: A Gathering of Favourites from our Picture Galleries, beautifully engraved on Steel. With Notices of the Artists by SYDNEY ARMYTAGE, M.A. Imperial 4to, cloth extra, gilt edges, 21s.

BECHSTEIN.—AS PRETTY AS SEVEN, and other German Stories. Collected by LUDWIG BECHSTEIN. With Additional Tales by the Brothers GRIMM, and 98 Illustrations by RICHTER. Square 8vo, cloth extra, 6s. 6d.; gilt edges, 7s. 6d.

BEERBOHM.—WANDERINGS IN PATAGONIA; or, Life among the Ostrich Hunters. By JULIUS BEERBOHM. With Illusts. Cr. 8vo, cl. extra, 3s. 6d.

BESANT (WALTER), NOVELS BY.
Cr. 8vo, cl. ex., 3s. 6d. each; post 8vo, illust. bds., 2s. each; cl. limp, 2s. 6d. each.
ALL SORTS AND CONDITIONS OF MEN. With Illustrations by FRED. BARNARD.
THE CAPTAINS' ROOM, &c. With Frontispiece by E. J. WHEELER.
ALL IN A GARDEN FAIR. With 6 Illustrations by HARRY FURNISS.
DOROTHY FORSTER. With Frontispiece by CHARLES GREEN.
UNCLE JACK, and other Stories. | CHILDREN OF GIBEON.
THE WORLD WENT VERY WELL THEN. With 12 Illustrations by A. FORESTIER.
HERR PAULUS: His Rise, his Greatness, and his Fall.
FOR FAITH AND FREEDOM. With Illustrations by A. FORESTIER and F. WADDY.

Crown 8vo, cloth extra, 3s. 6d. each.
TO CALL HER MINE, &c. With 9 Illustrations by A. FORESTIER.
THE BELL OF ST. PAUL'S.
ARMOREL OF LYONESSE: A Romance of To-day. With 12 Illusts. by F. BARNARD.
THE HOLY ROSE, &c. With Frontispiece by F. BARNARD.

ST. KATHERINE'S BY THE TOWER. With 12 full-page Illustrations by C. GREEN. Three Vols., crown 8vo.
FIFTY YEARS AGO. With 137 Plates and Woodcuts. Demy 8vo, cloth extra, 16s.
THE EULOGY OF RICHARD JEFFERIES. With Portrait. Cr. 8vo, cl. extra, 6s.
THE ART OF FICTION. Demy 8vo, 1s.

BESANT (WALTER) AND JAMES RICE, NOVELS BY.
Cr. 8vo, cl. ex., 3s. 6d. each; post 8vo, illust. bds., 2s. each; cl. limp, 2s. 6d. each.

READY-MONEY MORTIBOY.	BY CELIA'S ARBOUR.
MY LITTLE GIRL.	THE CHAPLAIN OF THE FLEET.
WITH HARP AND CROWN.	THE SEAMY SIDE.
THIS SON OF VULCAN.	THE CASE OF MR. LUCRAFT, &c.
THE GOLDEN BUTTERFLY.	'TWAS IN TRAFALGAR'S BAY, &c.
THE MONKS OF THELEMA.	THE TEN YEARS' TENANT, &c.

*** There is also a LIBRARY EDITION of the above Twelve Volumes, handsomely set in new type, on a large crown 8vo page, and bound in cloth extra, 6s. each.

BENNETT (W. C., LL.D.), WORKS BY. Post 8vo, cloth limp, 2s. each.
A BALLAD HISTORY OF ENGLAND. | SONGS FOR SAILORS.

BEWICK (THOMAS) AND HIS PUPILS. By AUSTIN DOBSON. With 95 Illustrations. Square 8vo, cloth extra, 6s.

BLACKBURN'S (HENRY) ART HANDBOOKS.
ACADEMY NOTES, separate years, from 1875-1887, 1889, and 1890, each 1s.
ACADEMY NOTES, 1891. With Illustrations. 1s.
ACADEMY NOTES, 1875-79. Complete in One Vol., with 600 Illusts. Cloth limp, 6s.
ACADEMY NOTES, 1880-84. Complete in One Vol., with 700 Illusts. Cloth limp, 6s.
GROSVENOR NOTES, 1877. 6d.
GROSVENOR NOTES, separate years, from 1878 to 1890, each 1s.
GROSVENOR NOTES, Vol. I., 1877-82. With 300 Illusts. Demy 8vo, cloth limp, 6s.
GROSVENOR NOTES, Vol. II., 1883-87. With 300 Illusts. Demy 8vo, cloth limp, 6s.
THE NEW GALLERY, 1888-1890. With numerous Illustrations, each 1s.
THE NEW GALLERY, 1891. With Illustrations. 1s.
ENGLISH PICTURES AT THE NATIONAL GALLERY. 114 Illustrations. 1s.
OLD MASTERS AT THE NATIONAL GALLERY. 128 Illustrations. 1s. 6d.
ILLUSTRATED CATALOGUE TO THE NATIONAL GALLERY. 242 Illusts. cl., 3s.
THE PARIS SALON, 1891. With Facsimile Sketches. 3s.
THE PARIS SOCIETY OF FINE ARTS, 1891. With Sketches. 3s. 6d.

BLAKE (WILLIAM): India-proof Etchings from his Works by WILLIAM BELL SCOTT. With descriptive Text. Folio, half-bound boards, 21s.

BLIND.—THE ASCENT OF MAN: A Poem. By MATHILDE BLIND. Crown 8vo, printed on hand-made paper, cloth extra, 5s.

BOURNE (H. R. FOX), WORKS BY.
ENGLISH MERCHANTS: Memoirs in Illustration of the Progress of British Commerce. With numerous Illustrations. Crown 8vo, cloth extra, 7s. 6d.
ENGLISH NEWSPAPERS: The History of Journalism. Two Vols., demy 8vo, cl., 25s.
THE OTHER SIDE OF THE EMIN PASHA RELIEF EXPEDITION. Crown 8vo, cloth extra, 6s.

BOWERS' (G.) HUNTING SKETCHES. Oblong 4to, hf.-bd. bds., 21s. each.
CANTERS IN CRAMPSHIRE. | LEAVES FROM A HUNTING JOURNAL.

BOYLE (FREDERICK), WORKS BY. Post 8vo, illustrated boards, 2s. each.
CHRONICLES OF NO-MAN'S LAND. | CAMP NOTES.
SAVAGE LIFE. Crown 8vo, cloth extra, 3s. 6d.; post 8vo, picture boards, 2s.

BRAND'S OBSERVATIONS ON POPULAR ANTIQUITIES; chiefly illustrating the Origin of our Vulgar Customs, Ceremonies, and Superstitions. With the Additions of Sir HENRY ELLIS, and Illustrations. Cr. 8vo, cloth extra, 7s. 6d.

BREWER (REV. DR.), WORKS BY.
THE READER'S HANDBOOK OF ALLUSIONS, REFERENCES, PLOTS, AND STORIES. Fifteenth Thousand. Crown 8vo, cloth extra, 7s. 6d.
AUTHORS AND THEIR WORKS, WITH THE DATES: Being the Appendices to "The Reader's Handbook," separately printed. Crown 8vo, cloth limp, 2s.
A DICTIONARY OF MIRACLES. Crown 8vo, cloth extra, 7s. 6d.

BREWSTER (SIR DAVID), WORKS BY. Post 8vo, cl. ex., 4s. 6d. each.
MORE WORLDS THAN ONE: Creed of Philosopher and Hope of Christian. Plates.
THE MARTYRS OF SCIENCE: GALILEO, TYCHO BRAHE, and KEPLER. With Portraits.
LETTERS ON NATURAL MAGIC. With numerous Illustrations.

BRET HARTE, WORKS BY.

LIBRARY EDITION, Complete in Six Volumes, crown 8vo, cloth extra, **6s.** each.
BRET HARTE'S COLLECTED WORKS. Arranged and Revised by the Author.
Vol. I. COMPLETE POETICAL AND DRAMATIC WORKS. With Steel Portrait.
Vol. II. LUCK OF ROARING CAMP—BOHEMIAN PAPERS—AMERICAN LEGENDS.
Vol. III. TALES OF THE ARGONAUTS—EASTERN SKETCHES.
Vol. IV. GABRIEL CONROY.
Vol. V. STORIES—CONDENSED NOVELS, &c.
Vol. VI. TALES OF THE PACIFIC SLOPE.

THE SELECT WORKS OF BRET HARTE, in Prose and Poetry. With Introductory Essay by J. M. BELLEW. Portrait of Author, and 50 Illusts. Cr. 8vo, cl. ex., **7s. 6d.**
BRET HARTE'S POETICAL WORKS. Hand-made paper & buckram. Cr. 8vo, **4s. 6d.**
THE QUEEN OF THE PIRATE ISLE. With 25 original Drawings by KATE GREENAWAY, reproduced in Colours by EDMUND EVANS. Small 4to, cloth, **5s.**

Crown 8vo, cloth extra, **3s. 6d.** each.
A WAIF OF THE PLAINS. With 60 Illustrations by STANLEY L. WOOD.
A WARD OF THE GOLDEN GATE. With 59 Illustrations by STANLEY L. WOOD.
A SAPPHO OF GREEN SPRINGS, &c. With Two Illustrations by HUME NISBET.
COLONEL STARBOTTLE'S CLIENT, &c. With Front. by F. BARNARD. [*Preparing*

Post 8vo, illustrated boards, **2s.** each.
GABRIEL CONROY. | THE LUCK OF ROARING CAMP, &c.
AN HEIRESS OF RED DOG, &c. | CALIFORNIAN STORIES.

Post 8vo, illustrated boards, **2s.** each; cloth limp, **2s. 6d.** each.
FLIP. | MARUJA. | A PHYLLIS OF THE SIERRAS.

Fcap. 8vo picture cover, **1s.** each.
THE TWINS OF TABLE MOUNTAIN. | JEFF BRIGGS'S LOVE STORY.

BRILLAT-SAVARIN.—GASTRONOMY AS A FINE ART. By BRILLAT-SAVARIN. Translated by R. E. ANDERSON, M.A. Post 8vo, half-bound, **2s.**

BRYDGES.—UNCLE SAM AT HOME. By HAROLD BRYDGES. Post 8vo, illustrated boards, **2s.**; cloth limp, **2s. 6d.**

BUCHANAN'S (ROBERT) WORKS. Crown 8vo, cloth extra, **6s.** each.
SELECTED POEMS OF ROBERT BUCHANAN. With Frontispiece by T. DALZIEL.
THE EARTHQUAKE; or, Six Days and a Sabbath.
THE CITY OF DREAM: An Epic Poem. With Two Illustrations by P. MACNAB.
THE OUTCAST: A Rhyme for the Time. With 12 Full-page Illustrations and numerous Vignettes. Crown 8vo, cloth extra, **8s.**
ROBERT BUCHANAN'S COMPLETE POETICAL WORKS. With Steel-plate Portrait. Crown 8vo, cloth extra, **7s. 6d.**

Crown 8vo, cloth extra, **3s. 6d.** each; post 8vo, illustrated boards, **2s.** each.
THE SHADOW OF THE SWORD. | LOVE ME FOR EVER. Frontispiece.
A CHILD OF NATURE. Frontispiece. | ANNAN WATER. | FOXGLOVE MANOR.
GOD AND THE MAN. With 11 Illustrations by FRED. BARNARD. | THE NEW ABELARD.
 | MATT: A Story of a Caravan. Front.
THE MARTYRDOM OF MADELINE. | THE MASTER OF THE MINE. Front.
With Frontispiece by A. W. COOPER. | THE HEIR OF LINNE.

BURTON (CAPTAIN).—THE BOOK OF THE SWORD: Being a History of the Sword and its Use in all Countries, from the Earliest Times. By RICHARD F. BURTON. With over 400 Illustrations. Square 8vo, cloth extra, **32s.**

BURTON (ROBERT).
THE ANATOMY OF MELANCHOLY: A New Edition, with translations of the Classical Extracts. Demy 8vo, cloth extra, **7s. 6d.**
MELANCHOLY ANATOMISED: Being an Abridgment, for popular use, of BURTON'S ANATOMY OF MELANCHOLY. Post 8vo, cloth limp, **2s. 6d.**

CAINE (T. HALL), NOVELS BY. Crown 8vo, cloth extra, **3s. 6d.** each post 8vo, illustrated boards, **2s.** each; cloth limp, **2s. 6d.** each.
SHADOW OF A CRIME. | A SON OF HAGAR. | THE DEEMSTER.

CAMERON (COMMANDER).—THE CRUISE OF THE "BLACK PRINCE" PRIVATEER. By V. LOVETT CAMERON, R.N., C.B. With Two Illustrations by P. MACNAB. Crown 8vo, cloth extra, **5s.**; post 8vo, illustrated boards, **2s.**

CAMERON (MRS. H. LOVETT), NOVELS BY.
Crown 8vo, cloth extra, **3s. 6d.** each; post 8vo, illustrated boards, **2s.** each.
JULIET'S GUARDIAN. | DECEIVERS EVER.

CARLYLE (THOMAS) ON THE CHOICE OF BOOKS. With Life by R. H. Shepherd, and Three Illustrations. Post 8vo, cloth extra, 1s. 6d.
THE CORRESPONDENCE OF THOMAS CARLYLE AND RALPH WALDO EMERSON, 1834 to 1872. Edited by Charles Eliot Norton. With Portraits. Two Vols., crown 8vo, cloth extra, 24s.

CARLYLE (JANE WELSH), LIFE OF. By Mrs. Alexander Ireland. With Portrait and Facsimile Letter. Small demy 8vo, cloth extra, 7s. 6d.

CHAPMAN'S (GEORGE) WORKS. Vol. I. contains the Plays complete, including the doubtful ones. Vol. II., the Poems and Minor Translations, with an Introductory Essay by Algernon Charles Swinburne. Vol. III., the Translations of the Iliad and Odyssey. Three Vols., crown 8vo, cloth extra, 6s. each.

CHATTO AND JACKSON.—A TREATISE ON WOOD ENGRAVING, Historical and Practical. By William Andrew Chatto and John Jackson. With an Additional Chapter by Henry G. Bohn, and 450 fine Illusts. Large 4to, hf.-bd., 28s.

CHAUCER FOR CHILDREN: A Golden Key. By Mrs. H. R. Haweis. With 8 Coloured Plates and 30 Woodcuts. Small 4to, cloth extra, 6s.
CHAUCER FOR SCHOOLS. By Mrs. H. R. Haweis. Demy 8vo, cloth limp, 2s. 6d.

CLARE.—FOR THE LOVE OF A LASS: A Tale of Tynedale. By Austin Clare. Post 8vo, picture boards, 2s.; cloth limp, 2s. 6d.

CLIVE (MRS. ARCHER), NOVELS BY. Post 8vo, illust. boards, 2s. each.
PAUL FERROLL. | WHY PAUL FERROLL KILLED HIS WIFE.

CLODD (EDW., F.R.A.S.).—MYTHS AND DREAMS. Cr. 8vo, cl. ex., 5s.

COBBAN.—THE CURE OF SOULS: A Story. By J. Maclaren Cobban. Post 8vo, illustrated boards, 2s.

COLEMAN (JOHN), WORKS BY.
PLAYERS AND PLAYWRIGHTS I HAVE KNOWN. Two Vols., 8vo, cloth, 24s.
CURLY: An Actor's Story. With 21 Illusts. by J. C. Dollman. Cr. 8vo, cl., 1s. 6d.

COLLINS (C. ALLSTON).—THE BAR SINISTER. Post 8vo, 2s.

COLLINS (MORTIMER AND FRANCES), NOVELS BY.
Crown 8vo, cloth extra, 3s. 6d. each; post 8vo, illustrated boards, 2s. each.
SWEET ANNE PAGE. | FROM MIDNIGHT TO MIDNIGHT. | TRANSMIGRATION.
BLACKSMITH AND SCHOLAR. | YOU PLAY ME FALSE. | VILLAGE COMEDY.
Post 8vo, illustrated boards, 2s. each.
A FIGHT WITH FORTUNE. | SWEET AND TWENTY. | FRANCES.

COLLINS (WILKIE), NOVELS BY.
Cr. 8vo, cl. ex., 3s. 6d. each; post 8vo, illust. bds., 2s. each; cl. limp, 2s. 6d. each.
ANTONINA. With a Frontispiece by Sir John Gilbert, R.A.
BASIL. Illustrated by Sir John Gilbert, R.A., and J. Mahoney.
HIDE AND SEEK. Illustrated by Sir John Gilbert, R.A., and J. Mahoney.
AFTER DARK. With Illustrations by A. B. Houghton.
THE DEAD SECRET. With a Frontispiece by Sir John Gilbert, R.A.
QUEEN OF HEARTS. With a Frontispiece by Sir John Gilbert, R.A.
THE WOMAN IN WHITE. With Illusts. by Sir J. Gilbert, R.A., and F. A. Fraser.
NO NAME. With Illustrations by Sir J. E. Millais, R.A., and A. W. Cooper.
MY MISCELLANIES. With a Steel-plate Portrait of Wilkie Collins.
ARMADALE. With Illustrations by G. H. Thomas.
THE MOONSTONE. With Illustrations by G. Du Maurier and F. A. Fraser.
MAN AND WIFE. With Illustrations by William Small.
POOR MISS FINCH. Illustrated by G. Du Maurier and Edward Hughes.
MISS OR MRS.? With Illusts. by S. L. Fildes, R.A., and Henry Woods, A.R.A.
THE NEW MAGDALEN. Illustrated by G. Du Maurier and C. S. Reinhardt.
THE FROZEN DEEP. Illustrated by G. Du Maurier and J. Mahoney.
THE LAW AND THE LADY. Illusts. by S. L. Fildes, R.A., and Sydney Hall.
THE TWO DESTINIES.
THE HAUNTED HOTEL. Illustrated by Arthur Hopkins.
THE FALLEN LEAVES. | HEART AND SCIENCE. | THE EVIL GENIUS.
JEZEBEL'S DAUGHTER. | "I SAY NO." | LITTLE NOVELS.
THE BLACK ROBE. | A ROGUE'S LIFE. | THE LEGACY OF CAIN.
BLIND LOVE. With Preface by Walter Besant, and Illusts. by A. Forestier.

COLLINS (CHURTON).—A MONOGRAPH ON DEAN SWIFT. By J. Churton Collins. Crown 8vo, cloth extra, 8s. [Shortly.

COLMAN'S HUMOROUS WORKS: "Broad Grins," "My Nightgown and Slippers," and other Humorous Works of GEORGE COLMAN. With Life by G. B. BUCKSTONE, and Frontispiece by HOGARTH. Crown 8vo, cloth extra, **7s. 6d.**

COLQUHOUN.—EVERY INCH A SOLDIER: A Novel. By M. J. COLQUHOUN. Post 8vo, illustrated boards, **2s.**

CONVALESCENT COOKERY: A Family Handbook. By CATHERINE RYAN. Crown 8vo, **1s.**; cloth limp, **1s. 6d.**

CONWAY (MONCURE D.), WORKS BY.
DEMONOLOGY AND DEVIL-LORE. With 65 Illustrations. Third Edition. Two Vols., demy 8vo, cloth extra, **28s.**
A NECKLACE OF STORIES. 25 Illusts. by W. J. HENNESSY. Sq. 8vo, cloth, **6s.**
PINE AND PALM: A Novel. Two Vols., crown 8vo, cloth extra, **21s.**
GEORGE WASHINGTON'S RULES OF CIVILITY Traced to their Sources and Restored. Fcap. 8vo, Japanese vellum, **2s. 6d.**

COOK (DUTTON), NOVELS BY.
PAUL FOSTER'S DAUGHTER. Cr. 8vo, cl. ex., **3s. 6d.**; post 8vo, illust. boards, **2s.**
LEO. Post 8vo, illustrated boards, **2s.**

CORNWALL.—POPULAR ROMANCES OF THE WEST OF ENGLAND; or, The Drolls, Traditions, and Superstitions of Old Cornwall. Collected by ROBERT HUNT, F.R.S. Two Steel-plates by GEO. CRUIKSHANK. Cr. 8vo, cl., **7s. 6d.**

CRADDOCK.—THE PROPHET OF THE GREAT SMOKY MOUNTAINS. By CHARLES EGBERT CRADDOCK. Post 8vo, illust. bds., **2s.**; cl. limp, **2s. 6d.**

CRUIKSHANK'S COMIC ALMANACK. Complete in TWO SERIES: The FIRST from 1835 to 1843; the SECOND from 1844 to 1853. A Gathering of the BEST HUMOUR of THACKERAY, HOOD, MAYHEW, ALBERT SMITH, A'BECKETT, ROBERT BROUGH, &c. With numerous Steel Engravings and Woodcuts by CRUIKSHANK, HINE, LANDELLS, &c. Two Vols, crown 8vo, cloth gilt, **7s. 6d.** each.
THE LIFE OF GEORGE CRUIKSHANK. By BLANCHARD JERROLD. With 84 Illustrations and a Bibliography. Crown 8vo, cloth extra, **7s. 6d.**

CUMMING (C. F. GORDON), WORKS BY. Demy 8vo, cl. ex., **8s. 6d.** each.
IN THE HEBRIDES. With Autotype Facsimile and 23 Illustrations.
IN THE HIMALAYAS AND ON THE INDIAN PLAINS. With 42 Illustrations.
VIA CORNWALL TO EGYPT. With Photogravure Frontis. Demy 8vo, cl., **7s. 6d.**

CUSSANS.—A HANDBOOK OF HERALDRY; with Instructions for Tracing Pedigrees and Deciphering Ancient MSS., &c. By JOHN E. CUSSANS. With 408 Woodcuts, Two Coloured and Two Plain Plates. Crown 8vo, cloth extra, **7s. 6d.**

CYPLES (W.)—HEARTS of GOLD. Cr. 8vo, cl., **3s. 6d.**; post 8vo, bds., **2s.**

DANIEL.—MERRIE ENGLAND IN THE OLDEN TIME. By GEORGE DANIEL. With Illustrations by ROBERT CRUIKSHANK. Crown 8vo, cloth extra, **3s. 6d.**

DAUDET.—THE EVANGELIST; or, Port Salvation. By ALPHONSE DAUDET. Crown 8vo, cloth extra. **3s. 6d.**; post 8vo, illustrated boards, **2s.**

DAVENANT.—HINTS FOR PARENTS ON THE CHOICE OF A PROFESSION FOR THEIR SONS. By F. DAVENANT, M.A. Post 8vo. **1s.**; cl., **1s. 6d.**

DAVIES (DR. N. E. YORKE-), WORKS BY.
Crown 8vo, **1s.** each; cloth limp, **1s. 6d.** each.
ONE THOUSAND MEDICAL MAXIMS AND SURGICAL HINTS.
NURSERY HINTS: A Mother's Guide in Health and Disease.
FOODS FOR THE FAT: A Treatise on Corpulency, and a Dietary for its Cure.
AIDS TO LONG LIFE. Crown 8vo, **2s.**; cloth limp, **2s. 6d.**

DAVIES' (SIR JOHN) COMPLETE POETICAL WORKS, including Psalms I. to L. in Verse, and other hitherto Unpublished MSS., for the first time Collected and Edited, with Memorial-Introduction and Notes, by the Rev. A. B. GROSART, D.D. Two Vols., crown 8vo, cloth boards. **12s.**

DAWSON.—THE FOUNTAIN OF YOUTH; A Novel of Adventure. By ERASMUS DAWSON, M.B. Edited by PAUL DEVON. With Two Illustrations by HUME NISBET. Crown 8vo, cloth extra, **3s. 6d.**

DE MAISTRE.—A JOURNEY ROUND MY ROOM. By XAVIER DE MAISTRE. Translated by HENRY ATTWELL. Post 8vo, cloth limp, 2s. 6d.

DE MILLE.—A CASTLE IN SPAIN. By JAMES DE MILLE. With a Frontispiece. Crown 8vo, cloth extra, 3s. 6d.; post 8vo, illustrated boards, 2s.

DERBY (THE).—THE BLUE RIBBON OF THE TURF: A Chronicle of the RACE FOR THE DERBY, from Diomed to Donovan. With Notes on the Winning Horses, the Men who trained them, Jockeys who rode them, and Gentlemen to whom they belonged; also Notices of the Betting and Betting Men of the period, and Brief Accounts of THE OAKS. By LOUIS HENRY CURZON. Cr. 8vo, cloth extra, 6s.

DERWENT (LEITH), NOVELS BY. Cr. 8vo cl., 3s. 6d. ea.; post 8vo, bds., 2s. ea.
OUR LADY OF TEARS. | CIRCE'S LOVERS.

DICKENS (CHARLES), NOVELS BY. Post 8vo, illustrated boards, 2s. each.
SKETCHES BY BOZ. | NICHOLAS NICKLEBY.
THE PICKWICK PAPERS. | OLIVER TWIST.
THE SPEECHES OF CHARLES DICKENS, 1841-1870. With a New Bibliography. Edited by RICHARD HERNE SHEPHERD. Crown 8vo, cloth extra, 6s.—Also a SMALLER EDITION, in the Mayfair Library, post 8vo, cloth limp, 2s. 6d.
ABOUT ENGLAND WITH DICKENS. By ALFRED RIMMER. With 57 Illustrations by C. A. VANDERHOOF, ALFRED RIMMER, and others. Sq. 8vo, cloth extra, 7s. 6d.

DICTIONARIES.
A DICTIONARY OF MIRACLES: Imitative, Realistic, and Dogmatic. By the Rev. E. C. BREWER, LL.D. Crown 8vo, cloth extra, 7s. 6d.
THE READER'S HANDBOOK OF ALLUSIONS, REFERENCES, PLOTS, AND STORIES. By the Rev. E. C. BREWER, LL.D. With an ENGLISH BIBLIOGRAPHY. Fifteenth Thousand. Crown 8vo, cloth extra, 7s. 6d.
AUTHORS AND THEIR WORKS, WITH THE DATES. Cr. 8vo, cloth limp, 2s.
FAMILIAR SHORT SAYINGS OF GREAT MEN. With Historical and Explanatory Notes. By SAMUEL A. BENT, A.M. Crown 8vo, cloth extra, 7s. 6d.
SLANG DICTIONARY: Etymological, Historical, and Anecdotal. Cr. 8vo, cl., 6s. 6d.
WOMEN OF THE DAY: A Biographical Dictionary. By F. HAYS. Cr. 8vo, cl., 5s.
WORDS, FACTS, AND PHRASES: A Dictionary of Curious, Quaint, and Out-of-the-Way Matters. By ELIEZER EDWARDS. Crown 8vo, cloth extra, 7s. 6d.

DIDEROT.—THE PARADOX OF ACTING. Translated, with Annotations, from Diderot's "Le Paradoxe sur le Comédien," by WALTER HERRIES POLLOCK. With a Preface by HENRY IRVING. Crown 8vo, parchment, 4s. 6d.

DOBSON (AUSTIN), WORKS BY.
THOMAS BEWICK & HIS PUPILS. With 95 Illustrations. Square 8vo, cloth, 6s.
FOUR FRENCHWOMEN: MADEMOISELLE DE CORDAY; MADAME ROLAND; THE PRINCESS DE LAMBALLE; MADAME DE GENLIS. Fcap. 8vo, hf. roxburghe, 2s. 6d.

DOBSON (W. T.), WORKS BY. Post 8vo, cloth limp, 2s. 6d. each.
LITERARY FRIVOLITIES, FANCIES, FOLLIES, AND FROLICS.
POETICAL INGENUITIES AND ECCENTRICITIES.

DONOVAN (DICK), DETECTIVE STORIES BY.
Post 8vo, illustrated boards, 2s. each; cloth limp, 2s. 6d. each.
THE MAN-HUNTER. | TRACKED AND TAKEN.
CAUGHT AT LAST! | WHO POISONED HETTY DUNCAN?
A DETECTIVE'S TRIUMPHS. [Preparing.
THE MAN FROM MANCHESTER. With 23 Illustrations. Crown 8vo, cloth, 6s.; post 8vo, illustrated boards, 2s.

DOYLE (A. CONAN, Author of "Micah Clarke"), NOVELS BY.
THE FIRM OF GIRDLESTONE. Crown 8vo, cloth extra, 6s.
STRANGE SECRETS. Told by CONAN DOYLE, PERCY FITZGERALD, FLORENCE MARRYAT, &c. Cr. 8vo, cl. ex., Eight Illusts. 6s.; post 8vo, illust. bds., 2s.

DRAMATISTS, THE OLD. With Vignette Portraits. Cr. 8vo, cl. ex., 6s. per Vol.
BEN JONSON'S WORKS. With Notes Critical and Explanatory, and a Biographical Memoir by WM. GIFFORD. Edited by Col. CUNNINGHAM. Three Vols.
CHAPMAN'S WORKS. Complete in Three Vols. Vol. I. contains the Plays complete; Vol. II., Poems and Minor Translations, with an Introductory Essay by A. C. SWINBURNE; Vol. III., Translations of the Iliad and Odyssey.
MARLOWE'S WORKS. Edited, with Notes, by Col. CUNNINGHAM. One Vol.
MASSINGER'S PLAYS. From GIFFORD's Text. Edit. by Col. CUNNINGHAM. One Vol.

DUNCAN (SARA JEANNETTE), WORKS BY.
A SOCIAL DEPARTURE: How Orthodocia and I Went round the World by Ourselves. With 111 Illustrations by F. H. TOWNSEND. Crown 8vo, cloth, **7s. 6d.**
AN AMERICAN GIRL IN LONDON. With 80 Illustrations by F. H. TOWNSEND. Crown 8vo, cloth extra, **7s. 6d.** *[Preparing.*

DYER.—THE FOLK-LORE OF PLANTS. By Rev. T. F. THISELTON DYER, M.A. Crown 8vo, cloth extra, **6s.**

EARLY ENGLISH POETS. Edited, with Introductions and Annotations, by Rev. A. B. GROSART, D.D. Crown 8vo, cloth boards, **6s.** per Volume.
FLETCHER'S (GILES) COMPLETE POEMS. One Vol.
DAVIES' (SIR JOHN) COMPLETE POETICAL WORKS. Two Vols.
HERRICK'S (ROBERT) COMPLETE COLLECTED POEMS. Three Vols.
SIDNEY'S (SIR PHILIP) COMPLETE POETICAL WORKS. Three Vols.

EDGCUMBE.—ZEPHYRUS: A Holiday in Brazil and on the River Plate. By E. R. PEARCE EDGCUMBE. With 41 Illustrations. Crown 8vo, cloth extra, **5s.**

EDWARDES (MRS. ANNIE), NOVELS BY:
A POINT OF HONOUR. Post 8vo, illustrated boards, **2s.**
ARCHIE LOVELL. Crown 8vo, cloth extra, **3s. 6d.**; post 8vo, illust. boards, **2s.**

EDWARDS (ELIEZER).—WORDS, FACTS, AND PHRASES: A Dictionary of Curious, Quaint, and Out-of-the-Way Matters. By ELIEZER EDWARDS. Crown 8vo, cloth extra, **7s. 6d.**

EDWARDS (M. BETHAM-), NOVELS BY.
KITTY. Post 8vo, illustrated boards, **2s.**; cloth limp, **2s. 6d.**
FELICIA. Post 8vo, illustrated boards, **2s.**

EGGLESTON (EDWARD).—ROXY: A Novel. Post 8vo, illust. bds., 2s.

EMANUEL.—ON DIAMONDS AND PRECIOUS STONES: Their History, Value, and Properties; with Simple Tests for ascertaining their Reality. By HARRY EMANUEL, F.R.G.S. With Illustrations, tinted and plain. Cr. 8vo, cl. ex., **6s.**

ENGLISHMAN'S HOUSE, THE: A Practical Guide to all interested in Selecting or Building a House; with Estimates of Cost, Quantities, &c. By C. J. RICHARDSON. With Coloured Frontispiece and 600 Illusts. Crown 8vo, cloth, **7s. 6d.**

EWALD (ALEX. CHARLES, F.S.A.), WORKS BY.
THE LIFE AND TIMES OF PRINCE CHARLES STUART, Count of Albany (THE YOUNG PRETENDER). With a Portrait. Crown 8vo, cloth extra, **7s. 6d.**
STORIES FROM THE STATE PAPERS. With an Autotype. Crown 8vo, cloth, **6s.**

EYES, OUR: How to Preserve Them from Infancy to Old Age. By JOHN BROWNING, F.R.A.S. With 70 Illusts. Eighteenth Thousand. Crown 8vo, **1s.**

FAMILIAR SHORT SAYINGS OF GREAT MEN. By SAMUEL ARTHUR BENT, A.M. Fifth Edition, Revised and Enlarged. Crown 8vo, cloth extra, **7s. 6d.**

FARADAY (MICHAEL), WORKS BY. Post 8vo, cloth extra, **4s. 6d.** each.
THE CHEMICAL HISTORY OF A CANDLE: Lectures delivered before a Juvenile Audience. Edited by WILLIAM CROOKES, F.C.S. With numerous Illustrations.
ON THE VARIOUS FORCES OF NATURE, AND THEIR RELATIONS TO EACH OTHER. Edited by WILLIAM CROOKES, F.C.S. With Illustrations.

FARRER (J. ANSON), WORKS BY.
MILITARY MANNERS AND CUSTOMS. Crown 8vo, cloth extra, **6s.**
WAR: Three Essays, reprinted from "Military Manners." Cr. 8vo, **1s.**; cl., **1s. 6d.**

FICTION.—A CATALOGUE OF NEARLY SIX HUNDRED WORKS OF FICTION published by CHATTO & WINDUS, with a Short Critical Notice of each (40 pages, demy 8vo), will be sent free upon application.

FIN-BEC.—THE CUPBOARD PAPERS: Observations on the Art of Living and Dining. By FIN-BEC. Post 8vo, cloth limp, **2s. 6d.**

FIREWORKS, THE COMPLETE ART OF MAKING; or, The Pyrotechnist's Treasury. By THOMAS KENTISH. With 267 Illustrations. Cr. 8vo, cl., **5s.**

FITZGERALD (PERCY, M.A., F.S.A.), WORKS BY.
THE WORLD BEHIND THE SCENES. Crown 8vo, cloth extra, 3s. 6d.
LITTLE ESSAYS: Passages from Letters of CHARLES LAMB. Post 8vo, cl., 2s. 6d.
A DAY'S TOUR: Journey through France and Belgium. With Sketches. Cr. 4to, 1s.
FATAL ZERO. Crown 8vo, cloth extra, 3s. 6d.; post 8vo, illustrated boards, 2s.

Post 8vo, illustrated boards, 2s. each.
BELLA DONNA. | LADY OF BRANTOME. | THE SECOND MRS. TILLOTSON.
POLLY. | NEVER FORGOTTEN. | SEVENTY-FIVE BROOKE STREET.

LIFE OF JAMES BOSWELL (of Auchinleck). With an Account of his Sayings, Doings, and Writings; and Four Portraits. Two Vols., demy 8vo, cloth extra, 24s. [*Preparing.*

FLETCHER'S (GILES, B.D.) COMPLETE POEMS: Christ's Victorie in Heaven, Christ's Victorie on Earth, Christ's Triumph over Death, and Minor Poems. With Notes by Rev. A. B. GROSART, D.D. Crown 8vo, cloth boards, 6s.

FLUDYER (HARRY) AT CAMBRIDGE: A Series of Family Letters. Post 8vo, picture cover, 1s.; cloth limp, 1s. 6d.

FONBLANQUE (ALBANY).—FILTHY LUCRE. Post 8vo, illust. bds., 2s.

FRANCILLON (R. E.), NOVELS BY.
Crown 8vo, cloth extra, 3s. 6d. each; post 8vo, illustrated boards, 2s. each.
ONE BY ONE. | QUEEN COPHETUA. | A REAL QUEEN. | KING OR KNAVE?
OLYMPIA. Post 8vo, illust. bds., 2s. | ESTHER'S GLOVE. Fcap. 8vo, pict. cover, 1s.
ROMANCES OF THE LAW. Crown 8vo, cloth, 6s.; post 8vo, illust. boards, 2s.

FREDERIC (HAROLD), NOVELS BY.
SETH'S BROTHER'S WIFE. Post 8vo, illustrated boards, 2s.
THE LAWTON GIRL. With Frontispiece by F. BARNARD. Cr. 8vo, cloth ex., 6s.; post 8vo, illustrated boards, 2s.

FRENCH LITERATURE, A HISTORY OF. By HENRY VAN LAUN. Three Vols., demy 8vo, cloth boards, 7s. 6d. each.

FRENZENY.—FIFTY YEARS ON THE TRAIL: Adventures of JOHN Y. NELSON, Scout, Guide, and Interpreter. By HARRINGTON O'REILLY. With 100 Illustrations by PAUL FRENZENY. Crown 8vo, cloth extra, 3s. 6d.

FRERE.—PANDURANG HARI; or, Memoirs of a Hindoo. With Preface by Sir BARTLE FRERE. Crown 8vo, cloth, 3s. 6d., post 8vo, illust. bds., 2s.

FRISWELL (HAIN).—ONE OF TWO: A Novel. Post 8vo, illust. bds., 2s.

FROST (THOMAS), WORKS BY. Crown 8vo, cloth extra, 3s. 6d. each.
CIRCUS LIFE AND CIRCUS CELEBRITIES. | LIVES OF THE CONJURERS.
THE OLD SHOWMEN AND THE OLD LONDON FAIRS.

FRY'S (HERBERT) ROYAL GUIDE TO THE LONDON CHARITIES. Showing their Name, Date of Foundation, Objects, Income, Officials, &c. Edited by JOHN LANE. Published Annually. Crown 8vo, cloth, 1s. 6d.

GARDENING BOOKS. Post 8vo, 1s. each; cloth limp, 1s. 6d. each.
A YEAR'S WORK IN GARDEN AND GREENHOUSE: Practical Advice as to the Management of the Flower, Fruit, and Frame Garden. By GEORGE GLENNY.
OUR KITCHEN GARDEN: Plants, and How we Cook Them. By TOM JERROLD.
HOUSEHOLD HORTICULTURE. By TOM and JANE JERROLD. Illustrated.
THE GARDEN THAT PAID THE RENT. By TOM JERROLD.

MY GARDEN WILD, AND WHAT I GREW THERE. By FRANCIS G. HEATH. Crown 8vo, cloth extra, gilt edges, 6s.

GARRETT.—THE CAPEL GIRLS: A Novel. By EDWARD GARRETT. Crown 8vo, cloth extra, 3s. 6d.; post 8vo, illustrated boards, 2s.

GENTLEMAN'S MAGAZINE, THE. 1s. Monthly. In addition to the Articles upon subjects in Literature, Science, and Art, for which this Magazine has so high a reputation, "TABLE TALK" by SYLVANUS URBAN appears monthly.
⁎* *Bound Volumes for recent years kept in stock,* 8s. 6d. *each Cases for binding,* 2s.

GENTLEMAN'S ANNUAL, THE. Published Annually in November. 1s.

GERMAN POPULAR STORIES. Collected by the Brothers GRIMM and Translated by EDGAR TAYLOR. With Introduction by JOHN RUSKIN, and 22 Steel Plates by GEORGE CRUIKSHANK. Square 8vo, cloth, 6s. 6d.; gilt edges, 7s. 6d.

GIBBON (CHARLES), NOVELS BY. Crown 8vo, cloth extra, 3s. 6d. each; post 8vo, illustrated boards, 2s. each.
ROBIN GRAY. | LOVING A DREAM. | OF HIGH DEGREE.
THE FLOWER OF THE FOREST. | IN HONOUR BOUND.
THE GOLDEN SHAFT.

Post 8vo, illustrated boards, 2s. each.
THE DEAD HEART. | IN LOVE AND WAR.
FOR LACK OF GOLD. | A HEART'S PROBLEM.
WHAT WILL THE WORLD SAY? | BY MEAD AND STREAM.
FOR THE KING. | THE BRAES OF YARROW.
QUEEN OF THE MEADOW. | FANCY FREE. | A HARD KNOT.
IN PASTURES GREEN. | HEART'S DELIGHT. | BLOOD-MONEY.

GIBNEY (SOMERVILLE).—SENTENCED! Cr. 8vo, 1s.; cl., 1s. 6d.

GILBERT (WILLIAM), NOVELS BY. Post 8vo, illustrated boards, 2s. each.
DR. AUSTIN'S GUESTS. | JAMES DUKE, COSTERMONGER.
THE WIZARD OF THE MOUNTAIN. |

GILBERT (W. S.), ORIGINAL PLAYS BY. In Two Series, each complete in itself, price 2s. 6d. each.
The FIRST SERIES contains: The Wicked World—Pygmalion and Galatea—Charity—The Princess—The Palace of Truth—Trial by Jury.
The SECOND SERIES: Broken Hearts—Engaged—Sweethearts—Gretchen—Dan'l Druce—Tom Cobb—H.M.S. "Pinafore"—The Sorcerer—Pirates of Penzance.
EIGHT ORIGINAL COMIC OPERAS written by W. S. GILBERT. Containing: The Sorcerer—H.M.S. "Pinafore"—Pirates of Penzance—Iolanthe—Patience—Princess Ida—The Mikado—Trial by Jury. Demy 8vo, cloth limp, 2s. 6d.
THE "GILBERT AND SULLIVAN" BIRTHDAY BOOK: Quotations for Every Day in the Year, Selected from Plays by W. S. GILBERT set to Music by Sir A. SULLIVAN. Compiled by ALEX. WATSON. Royal 16mo, Jap. leather, 2s. 6d.

GLANVILLE (ERNEST), NOVELS BY.
THE LOST HEIRESS: A Tale of Love, Battle and Adventure. With 2 Illusts. by HUME NISBET. Cr. 8vo, cloth extra, 3s. 6d.
THE FOSSICKER. With a Frontispiece. Crown 8vo, cloth extra, 3s. 6d.

GLENNY.—A YEAR'S WORK IN GARDEN AND GREENHOUSE: Practical Advice to Amateur Gardeners as to the Management of the Flower, Fruit, and Frame Garden. By GEORGE GLENNY. Post 8vo, 1s.; cloth limp, 1s. 6d.

GODWIN.—LIVES OF THE NECROMANCERS. By WILLIAM GODWIN. Post 8vo, cloth limp, 2s.

GOLDEN TREASURY OF THOUGHT, THE: An Encyclopædia of QUOTATIONS. Edited by THEODORE TAYLOR. Crown 8vo, cloth gilt, 7s. 6d.

GOWING.—FIVE THOUSAND MILES IN A SLEDGE: A Midwinter Journey Across Siberia. By LIONEL F. GOWING. With 30 Illustrations by C. J. UREN, and a Map by E. WELLER. Large crown 8vo, cloth extra, 8s.

GRAHAM.—THE PROFESSOR'S WIFE: A Story. By LEONARD GRAHAM. Fcap. 8vo, picture cover, 1s.

GREEKS AND ROMANS, THE LIFE OF THE, described from Antique Monuments. By ERNST GUHL and W. KONER. Edited by Dr. F. HUEFFER. With 545 Illustrations. Large crown 8vo, cloth extra, 7s. 6d.

GREENWOOD (JAMES), WORKS BY. Cr. 8vo, cloth extra, 3s. 6d. each.
THE WILDS OF LONDON. | LOW-LIFE DEEPS.

GREVILLE (HENRY), NOVELS BY:
NIKANOR. Translated by ELIZA E. CHASE. With 8 Illusts. Cr. 8vo, cl. extra, 6s.
A NOBLE WOMAN. Translated by ALBERT D. VANDAM. Crown 8vo, cloth extra, 5s.; post 8vo, illustrated boards, 2s.

HABBERTON (JOHN, Author of "Helen's Babies"**), NOVELS BY.** Post 8vo, illustrated boards 2s. each; cloth limp, 2s. 6d. each.
BRUETON'S BAYOU. | COUNTRY LUCK.

HAIR, THE: Its Treatment in Health, Weakness, and Disease. Translated from the German of Dr. J. Pincus. Crown 8vo, 1s.; cloth limp, 1s. 6d.

HAKE (DR. THOMAS GORDON), POEMS BY. Cr. 8vo, cl. ex., 6s. each.
NEW SYMBOLS. | LEGENDS OF THE MORROW. | **THE SERPENT PLAY.**
MAIDEN ECSTASY. Small 4to, cloth extra, 8s.

HALL.—SKETCHES OF IRISH CHARACTER. By Mrs. S. C. Hall. With numerous Illustrations on Steel and Wood by Maclise, Gilbert, Harvey, and George Cruikshank. Medium 8vo, cloth extra, 7s. 6d.

HALLIDAY (ANDR.).—EVERY-DAY PAPERS. Post 8vo, bds., 2s.

HANDWRITING, THE PHILOSOPHY OF. With over 100 Facsimiles and Explanatory Text. By Don Felix de Salamanca. Post 8vo, cloth limp, 2s. 6d.

HANKY-PANKY: A Collection of Very Easy Tricks, Very Difficult Tricks, White Magic, Sleight of Hand, &c. Edited by W. H. Cremer. With 200 Illustrations. Crown 8vo, cloth extra, 4s. 6d.

HARDY (LADY DUFFUS).—PAUL WYNTER'S SACRIFICE. By Lady Duffus Hardy. Post 8vo, illustrated boards, 2s.

HARDY (THOMAS).—UNDER THE GREENWOOD TREE. By Thomas Hardy, Author of "Far from the Madding Crowd." Post 8vo, illust. bds., 2s.

HARWOOD.—THE TENTH EARL. By J. Berwick Harwood. Post 8vo, illustrated boards, 2s.

HAWEIS (MRS. H. R.), WORKS BY. Square 8vo, cloth extra, 6s. each.
THE ART OF BEAUTY. With Coloured Frontispiece and 91 Illustrations.
THE ART OF DECORATION. With Coloured Frontispiece and 74 Illustrations.
CHAUCER FOR CHILDREN. With 8 Coloured Plates and 30 Woodcuts.
THE ART OF DRESS. With 32 Illustrations. Post 8vo, 1s.; cloth, 1s. 6d.
CHAUCER FOR SCHOOLS. Demy 8vo, cloth limp, 2s. 6d.

HAWEIS (Rev. H. R., M.A.).—AMERICAN HUMORISTS: Washington Irving, Oliver Wendell Holmes, James Russell Lowell, Artemus Ward, Mark Twain, and Bret Harte. Third Edition. Crown 8vo, cloth extra, 6s.

HAWLEY SMART.—WITHOUT LOVE OR LICENCE: A Novel. By Hawley Smart. Crown 8vo, cloth extra, 3s. 6d.

HAWTHORNE.—OUR OLD HOME. By Nathaniel Hawthorne. Annotated with Passages from the Author's Note-book, and Illustrated with 31 Photogravures. Two Vols., crown 8vo, buckram, gilt top, 15s.

HAWTHORNE (JULIAN), NOVELS BY.
Crown 8vo, cloth extra, 3s. 6d. each; post 8vo, illustrated boards, 2s. each.
GARTH. | ELLICE QUENTIN. | BEATRIX RANDOLPH. | DUST.
SEBASTIAN STROME. | DAVID POINDEXTER.
FORTUNE'S FOOL. | THE SPECTRE OF THE CAMERA.

Post 8vo, illustrated boards, 2s. each.
MISS CADOGNA. | LOVE—OR A NAME.
MRS. GAINSBOROUGH'S DIAMONDS. Fcap. 8vo, illustrated cover, 1s.
A DREAM AND A FORGETTING. Post 8vo, cloth limp, 1s. 6d.

HAYS.—WOMEN OF THE DAY: A Biographical Dictionary of Notable Contemporaries. By Frances Hays. Crown 8vo, cloth extra, 5s.

HEATH.—MY GARDEN WILD, AND WHAT I GREW THERE. By Francis George Heath. Crown 8vo, cloth extra, gilt edges, 6s.

HELPS (SIR ARTHUR), WORKS BY. Post 8vo, cloth limp, 2s. 6d. each.
ANIMALS AND THEIR MASTERS. | SOCIAL PRESSURE.
IVAN DE BIRON: A Novel. Cr. 8vo, cl. extra, 3s. 6d.; post 8vo, illust. bds., 2s.

HENDERSON.—AGATHA PAGE: A Novel. By Isaac Henderson. Crown 8vo, cloth extra, 3s. 6d.

HERMAN.—A LEADING LADY. By Henry Herman, joint-Author of "The Bishops' Bible." Post 8vo, cloth extra, 2s. 6d.

HERRICK'S (ROBERT) HESPERIDES, NOBLE NUMBERS, AND COMPLETE COLLECTED POEMS. With Memorial-Introduction and Notes by the Rev. A. B. GROSART, D.D.; Steel Portrait, &c. Three Vols., crown 8vo, cl. bds., 18s.

HERTZKA.—FREELAND: A Social Anticipation. By Dr. THEODOR HERTZKA. Translated by ARTHUR RANSOM. Crown 8vo, cloth extra, 6s.

HESSE-WARTEGG.—TUNIS: The Land and the People. By Chevalier ERNST VON HESSE-WARTEGG. With 22 Illustrations. Cr. 8vo, cloth extra, 3s. 6d.

HINDLEY (CHARLES), WORKS BY.
TAVERN ANECDOTES AND SAYINGS: Including the Origin of Signs, and Reminiscences connected with Taverns, Coffee Houses, Clubs, &c. With Illustrations. Crown 8vo, cloth extra, 3s. 6d.
THE LIFE AND ADVENTURES OF A CHEAP JACK. By ONE OF THE FRATERNITY. Edited by CHARLES HINDLEY. Crown 8vo, cloth extra, 3s. 6d.

HOEY.—THE LOVER'S CREED. By Mrs. CASHEL HOEY. Post 8vo, illustrated boards, 2s.

HOLLINGSHEAD (JOHN).—NIAGARA SPRAY. Crown 8vo, 1s.

HOLMES.—THE SCIENCE OF VOICE PRODUCTION AND VOICE PRESERVATION: A Popular Manual for the Use of Speakers and Singers. By GORDON HOLMES, M.D. With Illustrations. Crown 8vo, 1s.; cloth, 1s. 6d.

HOLMES (OLIVER WENDELL), WORKS BY.
THE AUTOCRAT OF THE BREAKFAST-TABLE. Illustrated by J. GORDON THOMSON. Post 8vo, cloth limp, 2s. 6d.—Another Edition, in sma' er type, with an Introduction by G. A. SALA. Post 8vo, cloth limp, 2s.
THE PROFESSOR AT THE BREAKFAST-TABLE. Post 8vo, cloth limp, 2s.

HOOD'S (THOMAS) CHOICE WORKS, in Prose and Verse. With Life of the Author, Portrait, and 200 Illustrations. Crown 8vo, cloth extra, 7s. 6d.
HOOD'S WHIMS AND ODDITIES. With 85 Illustrations. Post 8vo, printed on laid paper and half-bound, 2s.

HOOD (TOM).—FROM NOWHERE TO THE NORTH POLE: A Noah's Arkæological Narrative. By TOM HOOD. With 25 Illustrations by W. BRUNTON and E. C. BARNES. Square 8vo, cloth extra, gilt edges, 6s.

HOOK'S (THEODORE) CHOICE HUMOROUS WORKS; including his Ludicrous Adventures, Bons Mots, Puns, and Hoaxes. With Life of the Author, Portraits, Facsimiles, and Illustrations. Crown 8vo, cloth extra, 7s. 6d.

HOOPER.—THE HOUSE OF RABY: A Novel. By Mrs. GEORGE HOOPER. Post 8vo, illustrated boards, 2s.

HOPKINS.—"'TWIXT LOVE AND DUTY:" A Novel. By TIGHE HOPKINS. Post 8vo, illustrated boards, 2s.

HORNE.—ORION: An Epic Poem. By RICHARD HENGIST HORNE. With Photographic Portrait by SUMMERS. Tenth Edition. Cr. 8vo, cloth extra, 7s.

HORSE (THE) AND HIS RIDER: An Anecdotic Medley. By "THORMANBY." Crown 8vo, cloth extra, 6s.

HUNT.—ESSAYS BY LEIGH HUNT: A TALE FOR A CHIMNEY CORNER, and other Pieces. Edited, with an Introduction, by EDMUND OLLIER. Post 8vo, printed on laid paper and half-bd., 2s. Also in sm. sq. 8vo, cl. extra, at same price.

HUNT (MRS. ALFRED), NOVELS BY.
Crown 8vo, cloth extra, 3s. 6d. each; post 8vo, illustrated boards, 2s. each.
THE LEADEN CASKET. | SELF-CONDEMNED. | THAT OTHER PERSON.
THORNICROFT'S MODEL. Post 8vo, illustrated boards, 2

HYDROPHOBIA: An Account of M. PASTEUR'S System. Containing a Translation of all his Communications on the Subject, the Technique of his Method, and Statistics. By RENAUD SUZOR, M.B. Crown 8vo, cloth extra, 6s.

INGELOW (JEAN).—FATED TO BE FREE. With 24 Illustrations by G. J. PINWELL. Cr. 8vo, cloth extra, 3s. 6d.; post 8vo, illustrated boards, 2s.

INDOOR PAUPERS. By ONE OF THEM. Crown 8vo, 1s.; cloth, 1s. 6d.

IRISH WIT AND HUMOUR, SONGS OF. Collected and Edited by A. Perceval Graves. Post 8vo, cloth limp, 2s. 6d.

JAMES.—A ROMANCE OF THE QUEEN'S HOUNDS. By Charles James. Post 8vo, picture cover, 1s.; cloth limp, 1s. 6d.

JANVIER.—PRACTICAL KERAMICS FOR STUDENTS. By Catherine A. Janvier. Crown 8vo, cloth extra, 6s.

JAY (HARRIETT), NOVELS BY. Post 8vo, illustrated boards, 2s. each.
THE DARK COLLEEN. | THE QUEEN OF CONNAUGHT.

JEFFERIES (RICHARD), WORKS BY. Post 8vo, cloth limp, 2s. 6d. each.
NATURE NEAR LONDON. | THE LIFE OF THE FIELDS. | THE OPEN AIR.
THE EULOGY OF RICHARD JEFFERIES. By Walter Besant. Second Edition. With a Photograph Portrait. Crown 8vo, cloth extra, 6s.

JENNINGS (H. J.), WORKS BY.
CURIOSITIES OF CRITICISM. Post 8vo, cloth limp, 2s. 6d.
LORD TENNYSON: A Biographical Sketch. With a Photograph. Cr. 8vo, cl., 6s.

JEROME.—STAGELAND: Curious Habits and Customs of its Inhabitants. By Jerome K. Jerome. With 64 Illustrations by J. Bernard Partridge. Sixteenth Thousand. Fcap. 4to, cloth extra, 3s. 6d.

JERROLD.—THE BARBER'S CHAIR; & THE HEDGEHOG LETTERS. By Douglas Jerrold. Post 8vo, printed on laid paper and half-bound, 2s.

JERROLD (TOM), WORKS BY. Post 8vo, 1s. each; cloth limp, 1s. 6d. each.
THE GARDEN THAT PAID THE RENT.
HOUSEHOLD HORTICULTURE: A Gossip about Flowers. Illustrated.
OUR KITCHEN GARDEN: The Plants we Grow, and How we Cook Them.

JESSE.—SCENES AND OCCUPATIONS OF A COUNTRY LIFE. By Edward Jesse. Post 8vo, cloth limp, 2s.

JONES (WILLIAM, F.S.A.), WORKS BY. Cr. 8vo, cl. extra, 7s. 6d. each.
FINGER-RING LORE: Historical, Legendary, and Anecdotal. With nearly 300 Illustrations. Second Edition. Revised and Enlarged.
CREDULITIES, PAST AND PRESENT. Including the Sea and Seamen, Miners, Talismans, Word and Letter Divination, Exorcising and Blessing of Animals, Birds, Eggs, Luck, &c. With an Etched Frontispiece.
CROWNS AND CORONATIONS: A History of Regalia. With 100 Illustrations.

JONSON'S (BEN) WORKS. With Notes Critical and Explanatory, and a Biographical Memoir by William Gifford. Edited by Colonel Cunningham. Three Vols., crown 8vo, cloth extra, 6s. each.

JOSEPHUS, THE COMPLETE WORKS OF. Translated by Whiston. Containing "The Antiquities of the Jews" and "The Wars of the Jews." With 52 Illustrations and Maps. Two Vols., demy 8vo, half-bound, 12s. 6d.

KEMPT.—PENCIL AND PALETTE: Chapters on Art and Artists. By Robert Kempt. Post 8vo, cloth limp, 2s. 6d.

KERSHAW.—COLONIAL FACTS AND FICTIONS: Humorous Sketches. By Mark Kershaw. Post 8vo, illustrated boards, 2s.; cloth, 2s. 6d.

KEYSER.—CUT BY THE MESS: A Novel. By Arthur Keyser. Crown 8vo, picture cover, 1s.; cloth limp, 1s. 6d.

KING (R. ASHE), NOVELS BY. Cr. 8vo, cl., 3s. 6d. ea.; post 8vo, bds., 2s. ea.
A DRAWN GAME. | "THE WEARING OF THE GREEN."
PASSION'S SLAVE. Post 8vo, illustrated boards, 2s.
BELL BARRY. 2 vols., crown 8vo.

KINGSLEY (HENRY), NOVELS BY.
OAKSHOTT CASTLE. Post 8vo, illustrated boards, 2s.
NUMBER SEVENTEEN. Crown 8vo, cloth extra, 3s. 6d.

KNIGHTS (THE) OF THE LION: A Romance of the Thirteenth Century. Edited, with an Introduction, by the Marquess of Lorne, K.T. Cr. 8vo, cl. ex., 6s.

KNIGHT.—THE PATIENT'S VADE MECUM: How to Get Most Benefit from Medical Advice. By WILLIAM KNIGHT, M.R.C.S., and EDWARD KNIGHT, L.R.C.P. Crown 8vo, 1s.; cloth limp, 1s. 6d.

LAMB'S (CHARLES) COMPLETE WORKS, in Prose and Verse. Edited, with Notes and Introduction, by R. H. SHEPHERD. With Two Portraits and Facsimile of a page of the "Essay on Roast Pig." Cr. 8vo, cl. ex., 7s. 6d.
THE ESSAYS OF ELIA. Post 8vo, printed on laid paper and half-bound, 2s.
LITTLE ESSAYS: Sketches and Characters by CHARLES LAMB, selected from his Letters by PERCY FITZGERALD. Post 8vo, cloth limp, 2s. 6d.

LANDOR.—CITATION AND EXAMINATION OF WILLIAM SHAKSPEARE, &c., before Sir THOMAS LUCY, touching Deer-stealing, 19th September, 1582. To which is added, A CONFERENCE OF MASTER EDMUND SPENSER with the Earl of Essex, touching the State of Ireland, 1595. By WALTER SAVAGE LANDOR. Fcap. 8vo, half-Roxburghe, 2s. 6d.

LANE.—THE THOUSAND AND ONE NIGHTS, commonly called in England THE ARABIAN NIGHTS' ENTERTAINMENTS. Translated from the Arabic, with Notes, by EDWARD WILLIAM LANE. Illustrated by many hundred Engravings from Designs by HARVEY. Edited by EDWARD STANLEY POOLE. With a Preface by STANLEY LANE-POOLE. Three Vols., demy 8vo, cloth extra, 7s. 6d. each.

LARWOOD (JACOB), WORKS BY.
THE STORY OF THE LONDON PARKS. With Illusts. Cr. 8vo, cl. extra, 3s. 6d.
ANECDOTES OF THE CLERGY: The Antiquities, Humours, and Eccentricities of the Cloth. Post 8vo, printed on laid paper and half-bound, 2s.

Post 8vo, cloth limp, 2s. 6d. each.
FORENSIC ANECDOTES. | THEATRICAL ANECDOTES.

LEIGH (HENRY S.), WORKS BY.
CAROLS OF COCKAYNE. Printed on hand-made paper, bound in buckram, 5s.
JEUX D'ESPRIT. Edited by HENRY S. LEIGH. Post 8vo, cloth limp, 2s. 6d.

LEYS (JOHN).—THE LINDSAYS: A Romance. Post 8vo, illust. bds., 2s.

LIFE IN LONDON; or, The History of JERRY HAWTHORN and CORINTHIAN TOM. With CRUIKSHANK'S Coloured Illustrations. Crown 8vo, cloth extra, 7s. 6d. [New Edition preparing.

LINSKILL.—IN EXCHANGE FOR A SOUL. By MARY LINSKILL. Post 8vo, illustrated boards, 2s.

LINTON (E. LYNN), WORKS BY. Post 8vo, cloth limp, 2s. 6d. each.
WITCH STORIES. | OURSELVES: Essays on Women.

Crown 8vo, cloth extra, 3s. 6d. each; post 8vo, illustrated boards, 2s. each.
SOWING THE WIND. | UNDER WHICH LORD?
PATRICIA KEMBALL. | "MY LOVE!" | IONE.
ATONEMENT OF LEAM DUNDAS. | PASTON CAREW, Millionaire & Miser.
THE WORLD WELL LOST. |

Post 8vo, illustrated boards, 2s. each.
THE REBEL OF THE FAMILY. | WITH A SILKEN THREAD.

LONGFELLOW'S POETICAL WORKS. With numerous Illustrations on Steel and Wood. Crown 8vo, cloth extra, 7s. 6d.

LUCY.—GIDEON FLEYCE: A Novel. By HENRY W. LUCY. Crown 8vo, cloth extra, 3s. 6d.; post 8vo, illustrated boards, 2s.

LUSIAD (THE) OF CAMOENS. Translated into English Spenserian Verse by ROBERT FFRENCH DUFF. With 14 Plates. Demy 8vo, cloth boards, 18s.

MACALPINE (AVERY), NOVELS BY.
TERESA ITASCA, and other Stories. Crown 8vo, bound in canvas, 2s. 6d.
BROKEN WINGS. With 6 Illusts. by W. J. HENNESSY. Crown 8vo, cloth extra, 6s.

MACCOLL (HUGH), NOVELS BY.
MR. STRANGER'S SEALED PACKET. Second Edition. Crown 8vo, cl. extra, 5s.
EDNOR WHITLOCK. Crown 8vo cloth extra 6s.

McCARTHY (JUSTIN, M.P.), WORKS BY.

A HISTORY OF OUR OWN TIMES, from the Accession of Queen Victoria to the General Election of 1880. Four Vols. demy 8vo, cloth extra, 12s. each.—Also a POPULAR EDITION, in Four Vols., crown 8vo, cloth extra, 6s. each.—And a JUBILEE EDITION, with an Appendix of Events to the end of 1886, in Two Vols., large crown 8vo, cloth extra, 7s. 6d. each.

A SHORT HISTORY OF OUR OWN TIMES. One Vol., crown 8vo, cloth extra, 6s.—Also a CHEAP POPULAR EDITION, post 8vo, cloth limp, 2s. 6d.

A HISTORY OF THE FOUR GEORGES. Four Vols. demy 8vo, cloth extra, 12s. each. [Vols. I. & II. ready.

Crown 8vo, cloth extra, 3s. 6d. each; post 8vo, illustrated boards, 2s. each.
THE WATERDALE NEIGHBOURS. | MISS MISANTHROPE.
MY ENEMY'S DAUGHTER. | DONNA QUIXOTE.
A FAIR SAXON. | THE COMET OF A SEASON.
LINLEY ROCHFORD. | MAID OF ATHENS.
DEAR LADY DISDAIN. | CAMIOLA: A Girl with a Fortune.

"THE RIGHT HONOURABLE." By JUSTIN MCCARTHY, M.P., and Mrs. CAMPBELL-PRAED. Fourth Edition. Crown 8vo, cloth extra, 6s.

McCARTHY (JUSTIN H., M.P.), WORKS BY.

THE FRENCH REVOLUTION. Four Vols., 8vo, 12s. each. [Vols. I. & II. ready.
AN OUTLINE OF THE HISTORY OF IRELAND. Crown 8vo, 1s.; cloth, 1s. 6d.
IRELAND SINCE THE UNION: Irish History, 1798-1886. Crown 8vo, cloth, 6s.
ENGLAND UNDER GLADSTONE, 1880-85. Crown 8vo, cloth extra, 6s.
HAFIZ IN LONDON: Poems. Small 8vo, gold cloth, 3s. 6d.
HARLEQUINADE: Poems. Small 4to, Japanese vellum, 8s.
OUR SENSATION NOVEL. Crown 8vo, picture cover, 1s.; cloth limp, 1s. 6d.
DOOM! An Atlantic Episode. Crown 8vo, picture cover, 1s.
DOLLY: A Sketch. Crown 8vo, picture cover, 1s.; cloth limp, 1s. 6d.
LILY LASS: A Romance. Crown 8vo, picture cover, 1s.; cloth limp, 1s. 6d.

MACDONALD (GEORGE, LL.D.), WORKS BY.

WORKS OF FANCY AND IMAGINATION. Ten Vols., cl. extra, gilt edges, in cloth case, 21s. Or the Vols. may be had separately, in grolier cl., at 2s. 6d. each.
Vol. I. WITHIN AND WITHOUT.—THE HIDDEN LIFE.
,, II. THE DISCIPLE.—THE GOSPEL WOMEN.—BOOK OF SONNETS.—ORGAN SONGS.
,, III. VIOLIN SONGS.—SONGS OF THE DAYS AND NIGHTS.—A BOOK OF DREAMS.—ROADSIDE POEMS.—POEMS FOR CHILDREN.
,, IV. PARABLES.—BALLADS.—SCOTCH SONGS.
,, V. & VI. PHANTASTES: A Faerie Romance. | Vol. VII. THE PORTENT.
,, VIII. THE LIGHT PRINCESS.—THE GIANT'S HEART.—SHADOWS.
,, IX. CROSS PURPOSES.—THE GOLDEN KEY.—THE CARASOYN.—LITTLE DAYLIGHT.
,, X. THE CRUEL PAINTER.—THE WOW O' RIVVEN.—THE CASTLE.—THE BROKEN SWORDS.—THE GRAY WOLF.—UNCLE CORNELIUS.

THE COMPLETE POETICAL WORKS OF DR. GEORGE MACDONALD. Collected and arranged by the Author. Crown 8vo, buckram, 6s. [Shortly.

MACDONELL.—QUAKER COUSINS: A Novel. By AGNES MACDONELL.
Crown 8vo, cloth extra, 3s. 6d.; post 8vo, illustrated boards, 2s.

MACGREGOR.—PASTIMES AND PLAYERS: Notes on Popular
Games. By ROBERT MACGREGOR. Post 8vo, cloth limp, 2s. 6d.

MACKAY.—INTERLUDES AND UNDERTONES; or, Music at Twilight.
By CHARLES MACKAY, LL.D. Crown 8vo, cloth extra, 6s.

MACLISE PORTRAIT GALLERY (THE) OF ILLUSTRIOUS LITERARY CHARACTERS: 85 PORTRAITS; with Memoirs — Biographical, Critical, Bibliographical, and Anecdotal—illustrative of the Literature of the former half of the Present Century, by WILLIAM BATES, B.A. Crown 8vo, cloth extra, 7s. 6d.

MACQUOID (MRS.), WORKS BY. Square 8vo, cloth extra, 7s. 6d. each.
IN THE ARDENNES. With 50 Illustrations by THOMAS R. MACQUOID.
PICTURES AND LEGENDS FROM NORMANDY AND BRITTANY. With 34 Illustrations by THOMAS R. MACQUOID.
THROUGH NORMANDY. With 92 Illustrations by T. R. MACQUOID, and a Map.
THROUGH BRITTANY. With 35 Illustrations by T. R. MACQUOID, and a Map.
ABOUT YORKSHIRE. With 67 Illustrations by T. R. MACQUOID.

Post 8vo, illustrated boards, 2s. each.
THE EVIL EYE, and other Stories. | LOST ROSE.

MAGIC LANTERN, THE, and its Management: including full Practical Directions for producing the Limelight, making Oxygen Gas, and preparing Lantern Slides. By T. C. HEPWORTH. With 10 Illustrations. Cr. 8vo, **1s.**; cloth, **1s. 6d.**

MAGICIAN'S OWN BOOK, THE: Performances with Cups and Balls, Eggs, Hats, Handkerchiefs, &c. All from actual Experience. Edited by W. H. CREMER. With 200 Illustrations. Crown 8vo, cloth extra, **4s. 6d.**

MAGNA CHARTA: An Exact Facsimile of the Original in the British Museum, 3 feet by 2 feet, with Arms and Seals emblazoned in Gold and Colours, **5s.**

MALLOCK (W. H.), WORKS BY.
THE NEW REPUBLIC. Post 8vo, picture cover, **2s.**; cloth limp, **2s. 6d.**
THE NEW PAUL & VIRGINIA: Positivism on an Island. Post 8vo, cloth, **2s. 6d.**
POEMS. Small 4to, parchment, **8s.**
IS LIFE WORTH LIVING? Crown 8vo, cloth extra, **6s.**

MALLORY'S (SIR THOMAS) MORT D'ARTHUR: The Stories of King Arthur and of the Knights of the Round Table. (A Selection.) Edited by B. MONTGOMERIE RANKING. Post 8vo, cloth limp, **2s.**

MARK TWAIN, WORKS BY. Crown 8vo, cloth extra, **7s. 6d.** each.
THE CHOICE WORKS OF MARK TWAIN. Revised and Corrected throughout by the Author. With Life, Portrait, and numerous Illustrations.
ROUGHING IT, and INNOCENTS AT HOME. With 200 Illusts. by F. A. FRASER.
THE GILDED AGE. By MARK TWAIN and C. D. WARNER. With 212 Illustrations.
MARK TWAIN'S LIBRARY OF HUMOUR. With 197 Illustrations.
A YANKEE AT THE COURT OF KING ARTHUR. With 220 Illusts. by BEARD.

Crown 8vo, cloth extra (illustrated), **7s. 6d.** each; post 8vo, illust. boards, **2s.** each.
THE INNOCENTS ABROAD; or New Pilgrim's Progress. With 234 Illustrations. (The Two-Shilling Edition is entitled MARK TWAIN'S PLEASURE TRIP.)
THE ADVENTURES OF TOM SAWYER. With 111 Illustrations.
A TRAMP ABROAD. With 314 Illustrations.
THE PRINCE AND THE PAUPER. With 190 Illustrations.
LIFE ON THE MISSISSIPPI. With 300 Illustrations.
ADVENTURES OF HUCKLEBERRY FINN. With 174 Illusts. by E. W. KEMBLE.

THE STOLEN WHITE ELEPHANT, &c. Cr. 8vo, cl., **6s.**; post 8vo, illust. bds., **2s.**

MARLOWE'S WORKS. Including his Translations. Edited, with Notes and Introductions, by Col. CUNNINGHAM. Crown 8vo, cloth extra, **6s.**

MARRYAT (FLORENCE), NOVELS BY. Post 8vo, illust. boards, **2s.** each.
A HARVEST OF WILD OATS. | WRITTEN IN FIRE. | FIGHTING THE AIR.
OPEN! SESAME! Crown 8vo, cloth extra, **3s. 6d.**; post 8vo, picture boards, **2s.**

MASSINGER'S PLAYS. From the Text of WILLIAM GIFFORD. Edited by Col. CUNNINGHAM. Crown 8vo, cloth extra, **6s.**

MASTERMAN.—HALF-A-DOZEN DAUGHTERS: A Novel. By J. MASTERMAN. Post 8vo, illustrated boards, **2s.**

MATTHEWS.—A SECRET OF THE SEA, &c. By BRANDER MATTHEWS. Post 8vo, illustrated boards, **2s.**; cloth limp, **2s. 6d.**

MAYHEW.—LONDON CHARACTERS AND THE HUMOROUS SIDE OF LONDON LIFE. By HENRY MAYHEW. With Illusts. Crown 8vo, cloth, **3s. 6d.**

MENKEN.—INFELICIA: Poems by ADAH ISAACS MENKEN. With Biographical Preface, Illustrations by F. E. LUMMIS and F. O. C. DARLEY, and Facsimile of a Letter from CHARLES DICKENS. Small 4to, cloth extra, **7s. 6d.**

MEXICAN MUSTANG (ON A), through Texas to the Rio Grande. By A. E. SWEET and J. ARMOY KNOX. With 265 Illusts. Cr. 8vo, cloth extra, **7s. 6d.**

MIDDLEMASS (JEAN), NOVELS BY. Post 8vo, illust. boards, **2s.** each.
TOUCH AND GO. | MR. DORILLION.

MILLER.—PHYSIOLOGY FOR THE YOUNG; or, The House of Life: Human Physiology, with its application to the Preservation of Health. By Mrs. F. FENWICK MILLER. With numerous Illustrations. Post 8vo, cloth limp, **2s. 6d.**

MILTON (J. L.), WORKS BY. Post 8vo, 1s. each; cloth, 1s. 6d. each.
THE HYGIENE OF THE SKIN. With Directions for Diet, Soaps, Baths, &c.
THE BATH IN DISEASES OF THE SKIN.
THE LAWS OF LIFE, AND THEIR RELATION TO DISEASES OF THE SKIN.
THE SUCCESSFUL TREATMENT OF LEPROSY. Demy 8vo, 1s.

MINTO (WM.)—WAS SHE GOOD OR BAD? Cr. 8vo, 1s.; cloth, 1s. 6d.

MOLESWORTH (MRS.), NOVELS BY.
HATHERCOURT RECTORY. Post 8vo, illustrated boards, 2s.
THAT GIRL IN BLACK. Crown 8vo, picture cover, 1s.; cloth, 1s. 6d.

MOORE (THOMAS), WORKS BY.
THE EPICUREAN; and ALCIPHRON. Post 8vo, half-bound, 2s.
PROSE AND VERSE, Humorous, Satirical, and Sentimental, by THOMAS MOORE; with Suppressed Passages from the MEMOIRS OF LORD BYRON. Edited by R. HERNE SHEPHERD. With Portrait. Crown 8vo, cloth extra, 7s. 6d.

MUDDOCK (J. E.), STORIES BY.
STORIES WEIRD AND WONDERFUL. Post 8vo, illust. boards, 2s.; cloth, 2s. 6d.
THE DEAD MAN'S SECRET; or, The Valley of Gold: A Narrative of Strange Adventure. With a Frontispiece by F. BARNARD. Crown 8vo, cloth extra, 5s.; post 8vo, illustrated boards, 2s.

MURRAY (D. CHRISTIE), NOVELS BY.
Crown 8vo, cloth extra. 3s. 6d. each; post 8vo, illustrated boards. 2s. each.
A LIFE'S ATONEMENT. | A MODEL FATHER. | A BIT OF HUMAN NATURE.
JOSEPH'S COAT. | HEARTS. | FIRST PERSON SINGULAR.
COALS OF FIRE. | THE WAY OF THE | CYNIC FORTUNE.
VAL STRANGE. | WORLD. |
BY THE GATE OF THE SEA. Post 8vo, picture boards, 2s.
OLD BLAZER'S HERO. With Three Illustrations by A. McCORMICK. Crown 8vo, cloth extra, 6s.; post 8vo, illustrated boards, 2s.

MURRAY (D. CHRISTIE) & HENRY HERMAN, WORKS BY.
Crown 8vo, cloth extra, 6s. each; post 8vo, illustrated boards, 2s. each.
ONE TRAVELLER RETURNS.
PAUL JONES'S ALIAS. With 13 Illustrations by A. FORESTIER and G. NICOLET.
THE BISHOPS' BIBLE. Crown 8vo, cloth extra, 3s. 6d.

MURRAY.—A GAME OF BLUFF: A Novel   By HENRY MURRAY.
Post 8vo, picture boards, 2s.; cloth limp, 2s. 6d.

NISBET (HUME), BOOKS BY.
"BAIL UP!" A Romance of BUSHRANGERS AND BLACKS. Cr. 8vo, cl. ex., 3s. 6d.
LESSONS IN ART. With 21 Illustrations. Crown 8vo, cloth extra, 2s. 6d.

NOVELISTS.—HALF-HOURS WITH THE BEST NOVELISTS OF THE CENTURY. Edit. by H. T. MACKENZIE BELL. Cr. 8vo, cl., 3s. 6d. [Preparing.

O'CONNOR.—LORD BEACONSFIELD: A Biography. By T. P. O'CONNOR, M.P. Sixth Edition, with an Introduction. Crown 8vo, cloth extra, 5s.

O'HANLON (ALICE), NOVELS BY. Post 8vo, illustrated boards, 2s. each.
THE UNFORESEEN. | CHANCE? OR FATE?

OHNET (GEORGES), NOVELS BY.
DOCTOR RAMEAU. Translated by Mrs. CASHEL HOEY. With 9 Illustrations by E. BAYARD. Crown 8vo, cloth extra, 6s.; post 8vo, illustrated boards, 2s.
A LAST LOVE. Translated by ALBERT D. VANDAM. Crown 8vo, cloth extra, 5s.; post 8vo, illustrated boards, 2s.
A WEIRD GIFT. Translated by ALBERT D. VANDAM. Crown 8vo, cloth, 3s. 6d.

OLIPHANT (MRS.), NOVELS BY. Post 8vo, illustrated boards, 2s. each.
THE PRIMROSE PATH. | THE GREATEST HEIRESS IN ENGLAND.
WHITELADIES. With Illustrations by ARTHUR HOPKINS and HENRY WOODS, A.R.A. Crown 8vo, cloth extra, 3s. 6d.; post 8vo, illustrated boards, 2s.

O'REILLY (MRS.).—PHŒBE'S FORTUNES. Post 8vo, illust. bds., 2s.

O'SHAUGHNESSY (ARTHUR), POEMS BY.
LAYS OF FRANCE. Crown 8vo, cloth extra, 10s. 6d.
MUSIC AND MOONLIGHT. Fcap. 8vo, cloth extra, 7s. 6d.
SONGS OF A WORKER. Fcap. 8vo, cloth extra, 7s. 6d.

BOOKS PUBLISHED BY

OUIDA, NOVELS BY. Cr. 8vo, cl., 3s. 6d. each; post 8vo, illust. bds., 2s. each.

HELD IN BONDAGE.	FOLLE-FARINE.	MOTHS.
TRICOTRIN.	A DOG OF FLANDERS.	PIPISTRELLO.
STRATHMORE.	PASCAREL.	A VILLAGE COMMUNE.
CHANDOS.	TWO LITTLE WOODEN SHOES.	IN MAREMMA.
CECIL CASTLEMAINE'S GAGE.	SIGNA.	BIMBI.
IDALIA.	IN A WINTER CITY.	WANDA.
UNDER TWO FLAGS.	ARIADNE.	FRESCOES.
PUCK.	FRIENDSHIP.	PRINCESS NAPRAXINE.
		OTHMAR. | GUILDEROY.

Crown 8vo, cloth extra, 3s. 6d. each.

SYRLIN.   RUFFINO.

WISDOM, WIT, AND PATHOS, selected from the Works of OUIDA by F. SYDNEY MORRIS. Post 8vo, cloth extra, 5s.—CHEAP EDITION, illustrated boards, 2s.

PAGE (H. A.), WORKS BY.
THOREAU: His Life and Aims. With Portrait. Post 8vo, cloth limp, 2s. 6d.
ANIMAL ANECDOTES. Arranged on a New Principle. Crown 8vo, cloth extra, 5s.

PASCAL'S PROVINCIAL LETTERS. A New Translation, with Historical Introduction and Notes by T. M'CRIE, D.D. Post 8vo, cloth limp, 2s.

PAUL.—GENTLE AND SIMPLE. By MARGARET A. PAUL. With Frontispiece by HELEN PATERSON. Crown 8vo, cloth, 3s. 6d.; post 8vo, illust. boards, 2s.

PAYN (JAMES), NOVELS BY.
Crown 8vo, cloth extra, 3s. 6d. each; post 8vo, illustrated boards, 2s. each.

LOST SIR MASSINGBERD.	A GRAPE FROM A THORN.
WALTER'S WORD.	FROM EXILE.
LESS BLACK THAN WE'RE PAINTED.	SOME PRIVATE VIEWS.
	THE CANON'S WARD.
BY PROXY.	THE TALK OF THE TOWN.
HIGH SPIRITS.	HOLIDAY TASKS.
UNDER ONE ROOF.	GLOW-WORM TALES.
A CONFIDENTIAL AGENT.	THE MYSTERY OF MIRBRIDGE.

Post 8vo, illustrated boards, 2s. each.

HUMOROUS STORIES.	THE CLYFFARDS OF CLYFFE.
THE FOSTER BROTHERS.	FOUND DEAD.
THE FAMILY SCAPEGRACE.	GWENDOLINE'S HARVEST.
MARRIED BENEATH HIM.	A MARINE RESIDENCE.
BENTINCK'S TUTOR.	MIRK ABBEY.
A PERFECT TREASURE.	NOT WOOED, BUT WON.
A COUNTY FAMILY.	TWO HUNDRED POUNDS REWARD.
LIKE FATHER, LIKE SON.	THE BEST OF HUSBANDS.
A WOMAN'S VENGEANCE.	HALVES.
CARLYON'S YEAR.|CECIL'S TRYST.	FALLEN FORTUNES.
MURPHY'S MASTER.	WHAT HE COST HER.
AT HER MERCY.	KIT: A MEMORY. | FOR CASH ONLY.

Crown 8vo, cloth extra, 3s. 6d. each.

IN PERIL AND PRIVATION: Stories of MARINE ADVENTURE Re-told. With 17 Illustrations.
THE BURNT MILLION.   THE WORD AND THE WILL.
SUNNY STORIES, and some SHADY ONES. With a Frontispiece by FRED. BARNARD.
NOTES FROM THE "NEWS." Crown 8vo, portrait cover, 1s.; cloth, 1s. 6d.

PENNELL (H. CHOLMONDELEY), WORKS BY. Post 8vo, cl., 2s. 6d. each.
PUCK ON PEGASUS. With Illustrations.
PEGASUS RE-SADDLED. With Ten full-page Illustrations by G. DU MAURIER.
THE MUSES OF MAYFAIR. Vers de Société, Selected by H. C. PENNELL.

PHELPS (E. STUART), WORKS BY. Post 8vo, 1s. each; cloth, 1s. 6d. each.
BEYOND THE GATES. By the Author of "The Gates Ajar."
AN OLD MAID'S PARADISE.
BURGLARS IN PARADISE.

JACK THE FISHERMAN. Illustrated by C. W. REED. Cr. 8vo, 1s.; cloth, 1s. 6d.

PIRKIS (C. L.), NOVELS BY.
TROOPING WITH CROWS. Fcap. 8vo, picture cover, 1s.
LADY LOVELACE. Post 8vo, illustrated boards, 2s.

PLANCHE (J. R.), WORKS BY.
THE PURSUIVANT OF ARMS; or, Heraldry Founded upon Facts. With Coloured Frontispiece, Five Plates, and 209 Illusts. Crown 8vo, cloth, 7s. 6d.
SONGS AND POEMS, 1819-1879. Introduction by Mrs. MACKARNESS. Cr. 8vo, cl., 6s.

PLUTARCH'S LIVES OF ILLUSTRIOUS MEN. Translated from the Greek, with Notes Critical and Historical, and a Life of Plutarch, by JOHN and WILLIAM LANGHORNE. With Portraits. Two Vols., demy 8vo, half-bound, 10s. 6d.

POE'S (EDGAR ALLAN) CHOICE WORKS, in Prose and Poetry. Introduction by CHAS. BAUDELAIRE, Portrait, and Facsimiles. Cr 8vo, cloth, 7s. 6d.
THE MYSTERY OF MARIE ROGET, &c. Post 8vo, illustrated boards, 2s.

POPE'S POETICAL WORKS. Post 8vo, cloth limp, 2s.

PRICE (E. C.), NOVELS BY.
Crown 8vo, cloth extra, 3s. 6d. each; post 8vo, illustrated boards, 2s. each.
VALENTINA. | THE FOREIGNERS. | MRS. LANCASTER'S RIVAL.
GERALD. Post 8vo, illustrated boards, 2s.

PRINCESS OLGA.—RADNA; or, The Great Conspiracy of 1881. By the Princess OLGA. Crown 8vo, cloth extra, 6s.

PROCTOR (RICHARD A., B.A.), WORKS BY.
FLOWERS OF THE SKY. With 55 Illusts. Small crown 8vo, cloth extra, 3s. 6d.
EASY STAR LESSONS. With Star Maps for Every Night in the Year, Drawings of the Constellations, &c. Crown 8vo, cloth extra, 6s.
FAMILIAR SCIENCE STUDIES. Crown 8vo, cloth extra, 6s.
SATURN AND ITS SYSTEM. With 13 Steel Plates. Demy 8vo, cloth ex., 10s. 6d.
MYSTERIES OF TIME AND SPACE. With Illustrations. Cr. 8vo, cloth extra, 6s.
THE UNIVERSE OF SUNS. With numerous Illustrations. Cr. 8vo, cloth ex., 6s.
WAGES AND WANTS OF SCIENCE WORKERS. Crown 8vo, 1s. 6d.

PRYCE.—MISS MAXWELL'S AFFECTIONS. By RICHARD PRYCE, Author of "The Ugly Story of Miss Wetherby," &c. 2 vols., crown 8vo. [Shortly.

RAMBOSSON.—POPULAR ASTRONOMY. By J. RAMBOSSON, Laureate of the Institute of France. With numerous Illusts. Crown 8vo, cloth extra, 7s. 6d.

RANDOLPH.—AUNT ABIGAIL DYKES: A Novel. By Lt.-Colonel GEORGE RANDOLPH, U.S.A. Crown 8vo, cloth extra, 7s. 6d.

READE (CHARLES), NOVELS BY.
Crown 8vo, cloth extra, illustrated, 3s. 6d. each; post 8vo, illust. bds., 2s. each.
PEG WOFFINGTON. Illustrated by S. L. FILDES, R.A.—Also a POCKET EDITION, set in New Type, in Elzevir style, fcap. 8vo, half-leather, 2s. 6d.
CHRISTIE JOHNSTONE. Illustrated by WILLIAM SMALL.—Also a POCKET EDITION, set in New Type, in Elzevir style, fcap. 8vo, half-leather, 2s. 6d.
IT IS NEVER TOO LATE TO MEND. Illustrated by G. J. PINWELL.
THE COURSE OF TRUE LOVE NEVER DID RUN SMOOTH. Illustrated by HELEN PATERSON.
THE AUTOBIOGRAPHY OF A THIEF, &c. Illustrated by MATT STRETCH.
LOVE ME LITTLE, LOVE ME LONG. Illustrated by M. ELLEN EDWARDS.
THE DOUBLE MARRIAGE. Illusts. by Sir JOHN GILBERT, R.A., and C. KEENE.
THE CLOISTER AND THE HEARTH. Illustrated by CHARLES KEENE.
HARD CASH. Illustrated by F. W. LAWSON.
GRIFFITH GAUNT. Illustrated by S. L. FILDES, R.A., and WILLIAM SMALL.
FOUL PLAY. Illustrated by GEORGE DU MAURIER.
PUT YOURSELF IN HIS PLACE. Illustrated by ROBERT BARNES.
A TERRIBLE TEMPTATION. Illustrated by EDWARD HUGHES and A. W. COOPER.
A SIMPLETON. Illustrated by KATE CRAUFURD.
THE WANDERING HEIR. Illustrated by HELEN PATERSON, S. L. FILDES, R.A., C. GREEN, and HENRY WOODS, A.R.A.
A WOMAN-HATER. Illustrated by THOMAS COULDERY.
SINGLEHEART AND DOUBLEFACE. Illustrated by P. MACNAB.
GOOD STORIES OF MEN AND OTHER ANIMALS. Illustrated by E. A. ABBEY, PERCY MACQUOID, R.W.S., and JOSEPH NASH.
THE JILT, and other Stories. Illustrated by JOSEPH NASH.
READIANA. With a Steel-plate Portrait of CHARLES READE.
BIBLE CHARACTERS: Studies of David, Paul, &c. Fcap. 8vo, leatherette, 1s.

SELECTIONS FROM THE WORKS OF CHARLES READE. With an Introduction by Mrs. ALEX. IRELAND, and a Steel-Plate Portrait. Crown 8vo, buckram, 6s.

RIDDELL (MRS. J. H.), NOVELS BY.
Crown 8vo, cloth extra, 3s. 6d. each; post 8vo, illustrated boards, 2s. each.
HER MOTHER'S DARLING. | WEIRD STORIES.
THE PRINCE OF WALES'S GARDEN PARTY.
Post 8vo, illustrated boards, 2s. each.
UNINHABITED HOUSE. | FAIRY WATER. | MYSTERY IN PALACE GARDENS.

RIMMER (ALFRED), WORKS BY. Square 8vo, cloth gilt, 7s. 6d. each.
OUR OLD COUNTRY TOWNS. With 55 Illustrations.
RAMBLES ROUND ETON AND HARROW. With 50 Illustrations.
ABOUT ENGLAND WITH DICKENS. With 58 Illusts. by C. A. VANDERHOOF, &c.

ROBINSON CRUSOE. By DANIEL DEFOE. (MAJOR'S EDITION.) With 37 Illustrations by GEORGE CRUIKSHANK. Post 8vo, half-bound, 2s.

ROBINSON (F. W.), NOVELS BY.
Crown 8vo, cloth extra, 3s. 6d. each; post 8vo, illustrated boards, 2s. each.
WOMEN ARE STRANGE. | THE HANDS OF JUSTICE.

ROBINSON (PHIL), WORKS BY. Crown 8vo, cloth extra, 7s. 6d. each.
THE POETS' BIRDS. | THE POETS' BEASTS.
THE POETS AND NATURE: REPTILES, FISHES, INSECTS. [Preparing.

ROCHEFOUCAULD'S MAXIMS AND MORAL REFLECTIONS. With Notes, and an Introductory Essay by SAINTE-BEUVE. Post 8vo, cloth limp, 2s.

ROLL OF BATTLE ABBEY, THE: A List of the Principal Warriors who came from Normandy with William the Conqueror, and Settled in this Country, A.D. 1066-7. With Arms emblazoned in Gold and Colours. Handsomely printed. 5s.

ROWLEY (HON. HUGH), WORKS BY. Post 8vo, cloth, 2s. 6d. each.
PUNIANA: RIDDLES AND JOKES. With numerous Illustrations.
MORE PUNIANA. Profusely Illustrated.

RUNCIMAN (JAMES), STORIES BY.
Post 8vo, illustrated boards, 2s. each; cloth limp, 2s. 6d. each.
SKIPPERS AND SHELLBACKS. | GRACE BALMAIGN'S SWEETHEART.
SCHOOLS AND SCHOLARS.

RUSSELL (W. CLARK), BOOKS AND NOVELS BY:
Crown 8vo, cloth extra, 6s. each; post 8vo, illustrated boards, 2s. each.
ROUND THE GALLEY-FIRE. | A BOOK FOR THE HAMMOCK.
IN THE MIDDLE WATCH. | MYSTERY OF THE "OCEAN STAR."
A VOYAGE TO THE CAPE. | THE ROMANCE OF JENNY HARLOWE.
ON THE FO'K'SLE HEAD. Post 8vo, illustrated boards, 2s.
AN OCEAN TRAGEDY. Cr. 8vo, cloth extra, 3s. 6d.; post 8vo, illust. bds., 2s.
MY SHIPMATE LOUISE. Crown 8vo, cloth extra, 3s. 6d.

SAINT AUBYN (ALAN), NOVELS BY.
A FELLOW OF TRINITY. With a Note by OLIVER WENDELL HOLMES and a Frontispiece. Crown 8vo, cloth extra, 3s. 6d.; post 8vo, illust. boards, 2s.
THE JUNIOR DEAN. 3 vols., crown 8vo. [Shortly.

SALA.—GASLIGHT AND DAYLIGHT. By GEORGE AUGUSTUS SALA. Post 8vo, illustrated boards, 2s.

SANSON.—SEVEN GENERATIONS OF EXECUTIONERS: Memoirs of the Sanson Family (1688 to 1847). Crown 8vo, cloth extra, 3s. 6d.

SAUNDERS (JOHN), NOVELS BY.
Crown 8vo, cloth extra, 3s. 6d. each; post 8vo, illustrated boards, 2s. each.
GUY WATERMAN. | THE LION IN THE PATH. | THE TWO DREAMERS.
BOUND TO THE WHEEL. Crown 8vo, cloth extra, 3s. 6d.

SAUNDERS (KATHARINE), NOVELS BY.
Crown 8vo, cloth extra, 3s. 6d. each; post 8vo, illustrated boards, 2s. each.
MARGARET AND ELIZABETH. | HEART SALVAGE.
THE HIGH MILLS. | SEBASTIAN.
JOAN MERRYWEATHER. Post 8vo, illustrated boards, 2s.
GIDEON'S ROCK. Crown 8vo, cloth extra, 3s. 6d.

SCIENCE-GOSSIP: An Illustrated Medium of Interchange for Students and Lovers of Nature. Edited by Dr. J. E. TAYLOR, F.L.S., &c. Devoted to Geology, Botany, Physiology, Chemistry, Zoology, Microscopy, Telescopy, Physiography Photography, &c. Price 4d. Monthly; or 5s. per year, post-free. Vols. I. to XIX. may be had, 7s. 6d. each; Vols. XX. to date, 5s. each. Cases for Binding, 1s. 6d.

SECRET OUT, THE: One Thousand Tricks with Cards; with Entertaining Experiments in Drawing-room or "White Magic." By W. H. CREMER. With 300 Illustrations. Crown 8vo, cloth extra, 4s. 6d.

SEGUIN (L. G.), WORKS BY.
THE COUNTRY OF THE PASSION PLAY (OBERAMMERGAU) and the Highlands of Bavaria. With Map and 37 Illustrations. Crown 8vo, cloth extra, 3s. 6d.
WALKS IN ALGIERS. With 2 Maps and 16 Illusts. Crown 8vo, cloth extra, 6s.

SENIOR (WM.).—BY STREAM AND SEA. Post 8vo, cloth, 2s. 6d.

SHAKESPEARE, THE FIRST FOLIO.—MR. WILLIAM SHAKESPEARE'S COMEDIES, HISTORIES, AND TRAGEDIES. Published according to the true Originall Copies. London, Printed by ISAAC IAGGARD and ED. BLOUNT. 1623.—A reduced Photographic Reproduction. Small 8vo, half-Roxburghe, 7s. 6d.
SHAKESPEARE FOR CHILDREN: LAMB'S TALES FROM SHAKESPEARE. With Illustrations, coloured and plain, by J. MOYR SMITH. Crown 4to, cloth, 6s.

SHARP.—CHILDREN OF TO-MORROW: A Novel. By WILLIAM SHARP. Crown 8vo, cloth extra, 6s.

SHELLEY.—THE COMPLETE WORKS IN VERSE AND PROSE OF PERCY BYSSHE SHELLEY. Edited, Prefaced, and Annotated by R. HERNE SHEPHERD. Five Vols., crown 8vo, cloth boards, 3s. 6d. each.
POETICAL WORKS, in Three Vols.:
Vol. I. Introduction by the Editor; Posthumous Fragments of Margaret Nicholson; Shelley's Correspondence with Stockdale; The Wandering Jew; Queen Mab, with the Notes; Alastor, and other Poems; Rosalind and Helen; Prometheus Unbound; Adonais, &c.
Vol. II. Laon and Cythna; The Cenci; Julian and Maddalo; Swellfoot the Tyrant; The Witch of Atlas; Epipsychidion; Hellas.
Vol. III. Posthumous Poems; The Masque of Anarchy; and other Pieces.
PROSE WORKS, in Two Vols.:
Vol. I. The Two Romances of Zastrozzi and St. Irvyne; the Dublin and Marlow Pamphlets; A Refutation of Deism; Letters to Leigh Hunt, and some Minor Writings and Fragments.
Vol. II. The Essays; Letters from Abroad; Translations and Fragments, Edited by Mrs. SHELLEY. With a Bibliography of Shelley, and an Index of the Prose Works.

SHERARD.—ROGUES: A Novel. By R. H. SHERARD. Crown 8vo, picture cover, 1s.; cloth, 1s. 6d.

SHERIDAN (GENERAL). — PERSONAL MEMOIRS OF GENERAL P. H. SHERIDAN. With Portraits and Facsimiles. Two Vols., demy 8vo, cloth, 24s.

SHERIDAN'S (RICHARD BRINSLEY) COMPLETE WORKS. With Life and Anecdotes. Including his Dramatic Writings, his Works in Prose and Poetry, Translations, Speeches, Jokes, &c. With 10 Illusts. Cr. 8vo, cl., 7s. 6d.
THE RIVALS, THE SCHOOL FOR SCANDAL, and other Plays. Post 8vo, printed on laid paper and half-bound. 2s.
SHERIDAN'S COMEDIES: THE RIVALS and THE SCHOOL FOR SCANDAL. Edited, with an Introduction and Notes to each Play, and a Biographical Sketch, by BRANDER MATTHEWS. With Illustrations. Demy 8vo, half-parchment, 12s. 6d.

SIDNEY'S (SIR PHILIP) COMPLETE POETICAL WORKS, including all those in "Arcadia." With Portrait, Memorial-Introduction, Notes, &c. by the Rev. A. B. GROSART, D.D. Three Vols., crown 8vo, cloth boards, 18s.

SIGNBOARDS: Their History. With Anecdotes of Famous Taverns and Remarkable Characters. By JACOB LARWOOD and JOHN CAMDEN HOTTEN. With Coloured Frontispiece and 94 Illustrations. Crown 8vo, cloth extra, 7s. 6d.

SIMS (GEORGE R.), WORKS BY.
Post 8vo, illustrated boards, 2s. each; cloth limp, 2s. 6d. each.
ROGUES AND VAGABONDS. | MARY JANE MARRIED.
THE RING O' BELLS. | TALES OF TO-DAY.
MARY JANE'S MEMOIRS. | DRAMAS OF LIFE. With 60 Illustrations.
TINKLETOP'S CRIME. With a Frontispiece by MAURICE GREIFFENHAGEN.
Crown 8vo, picture cover, 1s. each; cloth, 1s. 6d. each.
HOW THE POOR LIVE; and HORRIBLE LONDON.
THE DAGONET RECITER AND READER: being Readings and Recitations in Prose and Verse, selected from his own Works by GEORGE R. SIMS.
DAGONET DITTIES. From the *Referee*.
THE CASE OF GEORGE CANDLEMAS.

SISTER DORA: A Biography. By MARGARET LONSDALE. With Four Illustrations. Demy 8vo, picture cover, 4d.; cloth, 6d.

BOOKS PUBLISHED BY

SKETCHLEY.—A MATCH IN THE DARK. By ARTHUR SKETCHLEY.
Post 8vo, illustrated boards, 2s.

SLANG DICTIONARY (THE): Etymological, Historical, and Anecdotal. Crown 8vo, cloth extra, 6s. 6d.

SMITH (J. MOYR), WORKS BY.
THE PRINCE OF ARGOLIS. With 130 Illusts. Post 8vo, cloth extra, 3s. 6d.
TALES OF OLD THULE. With numerous Illustrations. Crown 8vo, cloth gilt, 6s.
THE WOOING OF THE WATER WITCH. Illustrated. Post 8vo, cloth, 6s.

SOCIETY IN LONDON. By A FOREIGN RESIDENT. Crown 8vo. 1s.; cloth, 1s. 6d.

SOCIETY IN PARIS: The Upper Ten Thousand. A Series of Letters from Count PAUL VASILI to a Young French Diplomat. Crown 8vo, cloth, 6s.

SOMERSET. — SONGS OF ADIEU. By Lord HENRY SOMERSET. Small 4to, Japanese vellum, 6s.

SPALDING.—ELIZABETHAN DEMONOLOGY: An Essay on the Belief in the Existence of Devils. By T. A. SPALDING, LL.B. Crown 8vo, cloth extra, 5s.

SPEIGHT (T. W.), NOVELS BY.
Post 8vo, illustrated boards, 2s. each.
THE MYSTERIES OF HERON DYKE. | THE GOLDEN HOOP.
BY DEVIOUS WAYS, and A BARREN | HOODWINKED; and THE SANDY-
TITLE. | CROFT MYSTERY.

Post 8vo, cloth limp, 1s. 6d. each.
A BARREN TITLE. | WIFE OR NO WIFE?

THE SANDYCROFT MYSTERY. Crown 8vo, picture cover, 1s.

SPENSER FOR CHILDREN. By M. H. TOWRY. With Illustrations by WALTER J. MORGAN. Crown 4to, cloth gilt, 6s.

STARRY HEAVENS (THE): A POETICAL BIRTHDAY BOOK. Royal 16mo, cloth extra, 2s. 6d.

STAUNTON.—THE LAWS AND PRACTICE OF CHESS. With an Analysis of the Openings. By HOWARD STAUNTON. Edited by ROBERT B. WORMALD. Crown 8vo, cloth extra, 5s.

STEDMAN (E. C.), WORKS BY.
VICTORIAN POETS. Thirteenth Edition. Crown 8vo, cloth extra, 9s.
THE POETS OF AMERICA. Crown 8vo, cloth extra, 9s.

STERNDALE. — THE AFGHAN KNIFE: A Novel. By ROBERT ARMITAGE STERNDALE. Cr. 8vo, cloth extra, 3s. 6d.; post 8vo, illust. boards, 2s.

STEVENSON (R. LOUIS), WORKS BY. Post 8vo, cl. limp, 2s. 6d. each.
TRAVELS WITH A DONKEY. Eighth Edit. With a Frontis. by WALTER CRANE.
AN INLAND VOYAGE. Fourth Edition. With a Frontispiece by WALTER CRANE.

Crown 8vo, buckram, gilt top, 6s. each.
FAMILIAR STUDIES OF MEN AND BOOKS. Fifth Edition.
THE SILVERADO SQUATTERS. With a Frontispiece. Third Edition.
THE MERRY MEN. Second Edition. | UNDERWOODS: Poems. Fifth Edition.
MEMORIES AND PORTRAITS. Third Edition.
VIRGINIBUS PUERISQUE, and other Papers. Fifth Edition. | BALLADS.

NEW ARABIAN NIGHTS. Eleventh Edition. Crown 8vo, buckram, gilt top, 6s.; post 8vo, illustrated boards, 2s.
PRINCE OTTO. Post 8vo, illustrated boards, 2s.
FATHER DAMIEN: An Open Letter to the Rev. Dr. Hyde. Second Edition. Crown 8vo, hand-made and brown paper, 1s.

STODDARD. — SUMMER CRUISING IN THE SOUTH SEAS. By C. WARREN STODDARD. Illustrated by WALLIS MACKAY. Cr. 8vo, cl. extra, 3s. 6d.

STORIES FROM FOREIGN NOVELISTS. With Notices by HELEN and ALICE ZIMMERN. Crown 8vo, cloth extra, 3s. 6d.; post 8vo, illustrated boards, 2s.

STRANGE MANUSCRIPT (A) FOUND IN A COPPER CYLINDER.
With 19 Illustrations by GILBERT GAUL. Third Edition. Crown 8vo, cloth extra, 5s.

STRUTT'S SPORTS AND PASTIMES OF THE PEOPLE OF ENGLAND; including the Rural and Domestic Recreations, May Games, Mummeries, Shows, &c., from the Earliest Period to the Present Time. Edited by WILLIAM HONE. With 140 Illustrations. Crown 8vo, cloth extra, 7s. 6d.

SUBURBAN HOMES (THE) OF LONDON: A Residential Guide. With a Map, and Notes on Rental, Rates, and Accommodation. Crown 8vo, cloth, 7s. 6d.

SWIFT'S (DEAN) CHOICE WORKS, in Prose and Verse. With Memoir, Portrait, and Facsimiles of the Maps in "Gulliver's Travels." Cr. 8vo, cl., 7s. 6d.
GULLIVER'S TRAVELS, and **A TALE OF A TUB**. Post 8vo, printed on laid paper and half-bound, 2s.
A MONOGRAPH ON SWIFT. By J. CHURTON COLLINS. Cr. 8vo, cloth, 8s. [Shortly.

SWINBURNE (ALGERNON C.), WORKS BY.

SELECTIONS FROM POETICAL WORKS OF A. C. SWINBURNE. Fcap. 8vo, 6s.
ATALANTA IN CALYDON. Cr. 8vo, 6s.
CHASTELARD: A Tragedy. Cr. 8vo, 7s.
NOTES ON POEMS AND REVIEWS. Demy 8vo, 1s.
POEMS AND BALLADS. FIRST SERIES. Crown 8vo or fcap. 8vo, 9s.
POEMS AND BALLADS. SECOND SERIES. Crown 8vo or fcap. 8vo, 9s.
POEMS AND BALLADS. THIRD SERIES. Crown 8vo, 7s.
SONGS BEFORE SUNRISE. Crown 8vo, 10s. 6d.
BOTHWELL: A Tragedy. Crown 8vo, 12s. 6d.
SONGS OF TWO NATIONS. Cr. 8vo, 6s.
GEORGE CHAPMAN. (See Vol. II. of G. CHAPMAN'S Works.) Crown 8vo, 6s.
ESSAYS AND STUDIES. Cr. 8vo, 12s.
ERECHTHEUS: A Tragedy. Cr. 8vo, 6s.
SONGS OF THE SPRINGTIDES. Crown 8vo, 6s.
STUDIES IN SONG. Crown 8vo, 7s.
MARY STUART: A Tragedy. Cr. 8vo, 8s.
TRISTRAM OF LYONESSE. Cr. 8vo, 9s.
A CENTURY OF ROUNDELS. Sm. 4to, 8s.
A MIDSUMMER HOLIDAY. Cr. 8vo, 7s.
MARINO FALIERO: A Tragedy. Crown 8vo, 6s.
A STUDY OF VICTOR HUGO. Cr. 8vo, 6s.
MISCELLANIES. Crown 8vo, 12s.
LOCRINE: A Tragedy. Cr. 8vo, 6s.
A STUDY OF BEN JONSON. Cr. 8vo, 7s.

SYMONDS.—WINE, WOMEN, AND SONG: Mediæval Latin Students' Songs. With Essay and Trans. by J. ADDINGTON SYMONDS. Fcap. 8vo, parchment, 6s.

SYNTAX'S (DR.) THREE TOURS: In Search of the Picturesque, in Search of Consolation, and in Search of a Wife. With ROWLANDSON'S Coloured Illustrations, and Life of the Author by J. C. HOTTEN. Crown 8vo, cloth extra, 7s. 6d.

TAINE'S HISTORY OF ENGLISH LITERATURE. Translated by HENRY VAN LAUN. Four Vols., medium 8vo, cloth boards, 30s.—POPULAR EDITION, Two Vols., large crown 8vo, cloth extra, 15s.

TAYLOR'S (BAYARD) DIVERSIONS OF THE ECHO CLUB: Burlesques of Modern Writers. Post 8vo, cloth limp, 2s.

TAYLOR (DR. J. E., F.L.S.), WORKS BY. Cr. 8vo, cl. ex., 7s. 6d. each.
THE SAGACITY AND MORALITY OF PLANTS: A Sketch of the Life and Conduct of the Vegetable Kingdom. With a Coloured Frontispiece and 100 Illustrations.
OUR COMMON BRITISH FOSSILS, and Where to Find Them. 331 Illustrations.
THE PLAYTIME NATURALIST. With 366 Illustrations. Crown 8vo, cloth, 5s.

TAYLOR'S (TOM) HISTORICAL DRAMAS. Containing "Clancarty," "Jeanne Darc," "'Twixt Axe and Crown," "The Fool's Revenge," "Arkwright's Wife," "Anne Boleyn," "Plot and Passion." Crown 8vo, cloth extra, 7s. 6d.
*** The Plays may also be had separately, at 1s. each.

TENNYSON (LORD): A Biographical Sketch. By H. J. JENNINGS. With a Photograph-Portrait. Crown 8vo, cloth extra, 6s.

THACKERAYANA: Notes and Anecdotes. Illustrated by Hundreds of Sketches by WILLIAM MAKEPEACE THACKERAY, depicting Humorous Incidents in his School-life, and Favourite Characters in the Books of his Every-day Reading. With a Coloured Frontispiece. Crown 8vo, cloth extra, 7s. 6d.

THAMES.—A NEW PICTORIAL HISTORY OF THE THAMES. By A. S. KRAUSSE. With 340 Illustrations. Post 8vo, 1s.; cloth, 1s. 6d.

BOOKS PUBLISHED BY

THOMAS (BERTHA), NOVELS BY. Cr. 8vo, cl., **3s. 6d.** ea.; post 8vo, **2s.** ea.
CRESSIDA. | THE VIOLIN-PLAYER. | PROUD MAISIE.

THOMSON'S SEASONS, and CASTLE OF INDOLENCE. Introduction by ALLAN CUNNINGHAM, and Illustrations on Steel and Wood. Cr. 8vo, cl., **7s. 6d.**

THORNBURY (WALTER), WORKS BY. Cr. 8vo, cl. extra, **7s. 6d.** each.
THE LIFE AND CORRESPONDENCE OF J. M. W. TURNER. Founded upon Letters and Papers furnished by his Friends. With Illustrations in Colours.
HAUNTED LONDON. Edit. by E. WALFORD, M.A. Illusts. by F. W. FAIRHOLT, F.S.A.

Post 8vo, illustrated boards, **2s.** each.
OLD STORIES RE-TOLD. | TALES FOR THE MARINES.

TIMBS (JOHN), WORKS BY. Crown 8vo, cloth extra, **7s. 6d.** each.
THE HISTORY OF CLUBS AND CLUB LIFE IN LONDON: Anecdotes of its Famous Coffee-houses, Hostelries, and Taverns. With 42 Illustrations.
ENGLISH ECCENTRICS AND ECCENTRICITIES: Stories of Wealth and Fashion, Delusions, Impostures, and Fanatic Missions, Sporting Scenes, Eccentric Artists, Theatrical Folk, Men of Letters, &c. With 48 Illustrations.

TROLLOPE (ANTHONY), NOVELS BY.
Crown 8vo, cloth extra, **3s. 6d.** each; post 8vo, illustrated boards, **2s.** each.
THE WAY WE LIVE NOW. | MARION FAY.
KEPT IN THE DARK. | MR. SCARBOROUGH'S FAMILY.
FRAU FROHMANN. | THE LAND-LEAGUERS.

Post 8vo, illustrated boards, **2s.** each.
GOLDEN LION OF GRANPERE. | JOHN CALDIGATE. | AMERICAN SENATOR

TROLLOPE (FRANCES E.), NOVELS BY.
Crown 8vo, cloth extra, **3s. 6d.** each; post 8vo, illustrated boards, **2s.** each.
LIKE SHIPS UPON THE SEA. | MABEL'S PROGRESS. | ANNE FURNESS.

TROLLOPE (T. A.).—DIAMOND CUT DIAMOND. Post 8vo, illust. bds., **2s.**

TROWBRIDGE.—FARNELL'S FOLLY: A Novel. By J. T. TROWBRIDGE. Post 8vo, illustrated boards, **2s.**

TYTLER (C. C. FRASER-).—MISTRESS JUDITH: A Novel. By C. C. FRASER-TYTLER. Crown 8vo, cloth extra, **3s. 6d.**; post 8vo, illust. boards, **2s.**

TYTLER (SARAH), NOVELS BY.
Crown 8vo, cloth extra, **3s. 6d.** each; post 8vo, illustrated boards, **2s.** each.
THE BRIDE'S PASS. | BURIED DIAMONDS.
NOBLESSE OBLIGE. | THE BLACKHALL GHOSTS.
LADY BELL.

Post 8vo, illustrated boards, **2s.** each.
WHAT SHE CAME THROUGH. | BEAUTY AND THE BEAST.
CITOYENNE JACQUELINE. | DISAPPEARED.
SAINT MUNGO'S CITY. | THE HUGUENOT FAMILY.

VILLARI.—A DOUBLE BOND. By LINDA VILLARI. Fcap. 8vo, picture cover, **1s.**

WALT WHITMAN, POEMS BY. Edited, with Introduction, by WILLIAM M. ROSSETTI. With Portrait. Cr. 8vo, hand-made paper and buckram, **6s.**

WALTON AND COTTON'S COMPLETE ANGLER; or, The Contemplative Man's Recreation, by IZAAK WALTON; and Instructions how to Angle for a Trout or Grayling in a clear Stream, by CHARLES COTTON. With Memoirs and Notes by Sir HARRIS NICOLAS, and 61 Illustrations. Crown 8vo, cloth antique, **7s. 6d.**

WARD (HERBERT), WORKS BY.
FIVE YEARS WITH THE CONGO CANNIBALS. With 92 Illustrations by the Author, VICTOR PERARD, and W. B. DAVIS. Third ed. Roy. 8vo, cloth ex., **14s.**
MY LIFE WITH STANLEY'S REAR GUARD. With a Map by F. S. WELLER, F.R.G.S. Post 8vo, **1s.**; cloth, **1s. 6d.**

WARNER.—A ROUNDABOUT JOURNEY. By CHARLES DUDLEY WARNER. Crown 8vo, cloth extra, **6s.**

WALFORD (EDWARD, M.A.), WORKS BY.

WALFORD'S COUNTY FAMILIES OF THE UNITED KINGDOM (1891). Containing the Descent, Birth, Marriage, Education, &c., of 12,000 Heads of Families, their Heirs, Offices, Addresses, Clubs, &c. Royal 8vo, cloth gilt, 50s.

WALFORD'S SHILLING PEERAGE (1891). Containing a List of the House of Lords, Scotch and Irish Peers, &c. 32mo, cloth, 1s.

WALFORD'S SHILLING BARONETAGE (1891). Containing a List of the Baronets of the United Kingdom, Biographical Notices, Addresses, &c. 32mo, cloth, 1s.

WALFORD'S SHILLING KNIGHTAGE (1891). Containing a List of the Knights of the United Kingdom, Biographical Notices, Addresses, &c. 32mo, cloth, 1s.

WALFORD'S SHILLING HOUSE OF COMMONS (1891). Containing a List of all Members of Parliament, their Addresses, Clubs, &c. 32mo, cloth, 1s.

WALFORD'S COMPLETE PEERAGE, BARONETAGE, KNIGHTAGE, AND HOUSE OF COMMONS (1891). Royal 32mo, cloth extra, gilt edges 5s.

WALFORD'S WINDSOR PEERAGE, BARONETAGE, AND KNIGHTAGE (1891). Crown 8vo, cloth extra, 12s. 6d.

TALES OF OUR GREAT FAMILIES. Crown 8vo, cloth extra, 3s. 6d.

WILLIAM PITT: A Biography. Post 8vo, cloth extra, 5s.

WARRANT TO EXECUTE CHARLES I. A Facsimile, with the 59 Signatures and Seals. Printed on paper 22 in. by 14 in. 2s.

WARRANT TO EXECUTE MARY QUEEN OF SCOTS. A Facsimile, including Queen Elizabeth's Signature and the Great Seal. 2s.

WEATHER, HOW TO FORETELL THE, WITH POCKET SPECTROSCOPE. By F. W. CORY. With 10 Illustrations. Cr. 8vo, 1s.; cloth, 1s. 6d.

WESTROPP.—HANDBOOK OF POTTERY AND PORCELAIN. By HODDER M. WESTROPP. With Illusts. and List of Marks. Cr. 8vo, cloth, 4s. 6d.

WHIST.—HOW TO PLAY SOLO WHIST. By ABRAHAM S. WILKS and CHARLES F. PARDON. Crown 8vo, cloth extra, 3s. 6d.

WHISTLER'S (MR.) TEN O'CLOCK. Cr. 8vo, hand-made paper, 1s.

WHITE.—THE NATURAL HISTORY OF SELBORNE. By GILBERT WHITE, M.A. Post 8vo, printed on laid paper and half-bound, 2s.

WILLIAMS (W. MATTIEU, F.R.A.S.), WORKS BY.

SCIENCE IN SHORT CHAPTERS. Crown 8vo, cloth extra, 7s. 6d.

A SIMPLE TREATISE ON HEAT. With Illusts. Cr. 8vo, cloth limp, 2s. 6d.

THE CHEMISTRY OF COOKERY. Crown 8vo, cloth extra, 6s.

THE CHEMISTRY OF IRON AND STEEL MAKING. Crown 8vo, cloth extra, 9s.

WILLIAMSON.—A CHILD WIDOW. By Mrs. F. H. WILLIAMSON. Three Vols., crown 8vo.

WILSON (DR. ANDREW, F.R.S.E.), WORKS BY.

CHAPTERS ON EVOLUTION. With 259 Illustrations. Cr. 8vo, cloth extra, 7s. 6d.

LEAVES FROM A NATURALIST'S NOTE-BOOK. Post 8vo, cloth limp, 2s. 6d.

LEISURE-TIME STUDIES. With Illustrations. Crown 8vo, cloth extra, 6s.

STUDIES IN LIFE AND SENSE. With numerous Illusts. Cr. 8vo, cl. ex., 6s.

COMMON ACCIDENTS: HOW TO TREAT THEM. Illusts. Cr. 8vo, 1s.; cl., 1s. 6d.

GLIMPSES OF NATURE. With 35 Illustrations. Crown 8vo, cloth extra, 3s. 6d.

WINTER (J. S.), STORIES BY. Post 8vo, illustrated boards, 2s. each.
CAVALRY LIFE. | REGIMENTAL LEGENDS.

WISSMANN.—MY SECOND JOURNEY THROUGH EQUATORIAL AFRICA, from the Congo to the Zambesi, in 1886, 1887. By HERMANN VON WISSMANN. With a Map and 92 Illustrations. Demy 8vo, cloth extra, 16s.

WOOD.—SABINA: A Novel. By Lady WOOD. Post 8vo, boards, 2s.

WOOD (H. F.), DETECTIVE STORIES BY.
Crown 8vo, cloth extra, 6s. each; post 8vo, illustrated boards, 2s. each.
PASSENGER FROM SCOTLAND YARD. | ENGLISHMAN OF THE RUE CAIN.

WOOLLEY.—RACHEL ARMSTRONG; or, Love and Theology. By CELIA PARKER WOOLLEY. Post 8vo, illustrated boards, 2s.; cloth, 2s. 6d.

WRIGHT (THOMAS), WORKS BY. Crown 8vo, cloth extra, 7s. 6d. each.

CARICATURE HISTORY OF THE GEORGES. With 400 Pictures, Caricatures, Squibs, Broadsides, Window Pictures, &c.

HISTORY OF CARICATURE AND OF THE GROTESQUE IN ART, LITERATURE, SCULPTURE, AND PAINTING. Illustrated by F. W. FAIRHOLT, F.S.A.

YATES (EDMUND), NOVELS BY. Post 8vo, illustrated boards, 2s. each.
LAND AT LAST. | THE FORLORN HOPE. | CASTAWAY.

LISTS OF BOOKS CLASSIFIED IN SERIES.

. *For full cataloguing, see alphabetical arrangement, pp. 1-25.*

THE MAYFAIR LIBRARY.
Post 8vo, cloth limp, 2s. 6d. per Volume.

A Journey Round My Room. By XAVIER DE MAISTRE.
Quips and Quiddities. By W. D. ADAMS.
The Agony Column of "The Times."
Melancholy Anatomised: Abridgment of "Burton's Anatomy of Melancholy."
The Speeches of Charles Dickens.
Literary Frivolities, Fancies, Follies, and Frolics. By W. T. DOBSON.
Poetical Ingenuities. By W. T. DOBSON.
The Cupboard Papers. By FIN-BEC.
W. S. Gilbert's Plays. FIRST SERIES.
W. S. Gilbert's Plays. SECOND SERIES.
Songs of Irish Wit and Humour.
Animals and Masters. By Sir A. HELPS.
Social Pressure. By Sir A. HELPS.
Curiosities of Criticism. H. J. JENNINGS.
Holmes's Autocrat of Breakfast-Table.
Pencil and Palette. By R. KEMPT.
Little Essays: from LAMB's Letters.
Forensic Anecdotes. By JACOB LARWOOD.
Theatrical Anecdotes. JACOB LARWOOD.
Jeux d'Esprit. Edited by HENRY S. LEIGH.
Witch Stories. By E. LYNN LINTON.
Ourselves. By E. LYNN LINTON.
Pastimes & Players. By R. MACGREGOR.
New Paul and Virginia. W. H. MALLOCK.
New Republic. By W. H. MALLOCK.
Puck on Pegasus. By H. C. PENNELL.
Pegasus Re-Saddled. By H. C. PENNELL.
Muses of Mayfair. Ed. H. C. PENNELL.
Thoreau: His Life & Aims. By H. A. PAGE.
Puniana. By Hon. HUGH ROWLEY.
More Puniana. By Hon. HUGH ROWLEY.
The Philosophy of Handwriting.
By Stream and Sea. By WM. SENIOR.
Leaves from a Naturalist's Note-Book. By Dr. ANDREW WILSON.

THE GOLDEN LIBRARY.
Post 8vo, cloth limp, 2s. per Volume.

Bayard Taylor's Diversions of the Echo Club.
Bennett's Ballad History of England.
Bennett's Songs for Sailors.
Godwin's Lives of the Necromancers.
Pope's Poetical Works.
Holmes's Autocrat of Breakfast Table.
Holmes's Professor at Breakfast-Table.
Jesse's Scenes of Country Life.
Leigh Hunt's Tale for a Chimney Corner.
Mallory's Mort d'Arthur: Selections.
Pascal's Provincial Letters.
Rochefoucauld's Maxims & Reflections.

THE WANDERER'S LIBRARY.
Crown 8vo, cloth extra, 3s. 6d. each.

Wanderings in Patagonia. By JULIUS BEERBOHM. Illustrated.
Camp Notes. By FREDERICK BOYLE.
Savage Life. By FREDERICK BOYLE.
Merrie England in the Olden Time. By G. DANIEL. Illustrated by CRUIKSHANK.
Circus Life. By THOMAS FROST.
Lives of the Conjurers. THOMAS FROST.
The Old Showmen and the Old London Fairs. By THOMAS FROST.
Low-Life Deeps. By JAMES GREENWOOD.
Wilds of London. JAMES GREENWOOD.
Tunis. Chev. HESSE-WARTEGG. 22 Illusts.
Life and Adventures of a Cheap Jack.
World Behind the Scenes. P. FITZGERALD.
Tavern Anecdotes and Sayings.
The Genial Showman. By E. P. HINGSTON.
Story of London Parks. JACOB LARWOOD.
London Characters. By HENRY MAYHEW.
Seven Generations of Executioners.
Summer Cruising in the South Seas. By C. WARREN STODDARD. Illustrated.

POPULAR SHILLING BOOKS.

Harry Fludyer at Cambridge.
Jeff Briggs's Love Story. BRET HARTE.
Twins of Table Mountain. BRET HARTE.
A Day's Tour. By PERCY FITZGERALD.
Esther's Glove. By R. E. FRANCILLON.
Sentenced! By SOMERVILLE GIBNEY.
The Professor's Wife. By L. GRAHAM.
Mrs. Gainsborough's Diamonds. By JULIAN HAWTHORNE.
Niagara Spray. By J. HOLLINGSHEAD.
A Romance of the Queen's Hounds. By CHARLES JAMES.
The Garden that Paid the Rent. By TOM JERROLD.
Cut by the Mess. By ARTHUR KEYSER.
Our Sensation Novel. J. H. MCCARTHY.
Doom! By JUSTIN H. MCCARTHY, M.P.
Dolly. By JUSTIN H. MCCARTHY, M.P.
Lily Lass. JUSTIN H. MCCARTHY, M.P.
Was She Good or Bad? By W. MINTO.
That Girl in Black. Mrs. MOLESWORTH.
Notes from the "News." By JAS. PAYN.
Beyond the Gates. By E. S. PHELPS.
Old Maid's Paradise. By E. S. PHELPS.
Burglars in Paradise. By E. S. PHELPS.
Jack the Fisherman. By E. S. PHELPS.
Trooping with Crows. By C. L. PIRKIS.
Bible Characters. By CHARLES READE.
Rogues. By R. H. SHERARD.
The Dagonet Reciter. By G. R. SIMS.
How the Poor Live. By G. R. SIMS.
Case of George Candlemas. G. R. SIMS
Sandycroft Mystery. T. W. SPEIGHT.
Hoodwinked. By T. W. SPEIGHT.
Father Damien. By R. L. STEVENSON.
A Double Bond. By LINDA VILLARI.
My Life with Stanley's Rear Guard. By HERBERT WARD.

CHATTO & WINDUS, 214, PICCADILLY. 27

MY LIBRARY.

Choice Works, printed on laid paper, bound half-Roxburghe, 2s. 6d. each.

Four Frenchwomen. By AUSTIN DOBSON.
Citation and Examination of William Shakspeare. By W. S. LANDOR.
Christie Johnstone. By CHARLES READE. With a Photogravure Frontispiece.
Peg Woffington. By CHARLES READE.

THE POCKET LIBRARY.

Post 8vo, printed on laid paper and hf.-bd., 2s. each.

The Essays of Elia. By CHARLES LAMB.
Robinson Crusoe. Edited by JOHN MAJOR. With 37 Illusts. by GEORGE CRUIKSHANK.
Whims and Oddities. By THOMAS HOOD. With 85 Illustrations.
The Barber's Chair, and The Hedgehog Letters. By DOUGLAS JERROLD.
Gastronomy as a Fine Art. By BRILLAT-SAVARIN. Trans. R. E. ANDERSON, M.A.

The Epicurean, &c. By THOMAS MOORE.
Leigh Hunt's Essays. Ed. E. OLLIER.
The Natural History of Selborne. By GILBERT WHITE.
Gulliver's Travels, and The Tale of a Tub. By Dean SWIFT.
The Rivals, School for Scandal, and other Plays by RICHARD BRINSLEY SHERIDAN.
Anecdotes of the Clergy. J. LARWOOD.

THE PICCADILLY NOVELS.

LIBRARY EDITIONS OF NOVELS BY THE BEST AUTHORS, many Illustrated, crown 8vo, cloth extra, 3s. 6d. each.

By GRANT ALLEN.
Philistia.
Babylon.
In all Shades.
The Tents of Shem.
For Maimie's Sake.
The Devil's Die.
This Mortal Coil.
The Great Taboo.

By ALAN ST. AUBYN.
A Fellow of Trinity.

By Rev. S. BARING GOULD.
Red Spider. | Eve.

By W. BESANT & J. RICE.
My Little Girl.
Case of Mr. Lucraft.
This Son of Vulcan.
Golden Butterfly.
Ready-Money Mortiboy.
With Harp and Crown.
'Twas in Trafalgar's Bay.
The Chaplain of the Fleet.
By Celia's Arbour.
Monks of Thelema.
The Seamy Side.
Ten Years' Tenant.

By WALTER BESANT.
All Sorts and Conditions of Men.
The Captains' Room.
All in a Garden Fair.
The World Went Very Well Then.
For Faith and Freedom.
Dorothy Forster. | To Call Her Mine.
Uncle Jack. | The Holy Rose.
Children of Gibeon. | Armorel of Lyonesse.
Herr Paulus.
Bell of St. Paul's.

By ROBERT BUCHANAN.
The Shadow of the Sword.
A Child of Nature.
The Martyrdom of Madeline.
God and the Man. | The New Abelard.
Love Me for Ever. | Foxglove Manor.
Annan Water. | Master of the Mine.
Matt. | Heir of Linne.

By HALL CAINE.
The Shadow of a Crime.
A Son of Hagar. | The Deemster.

MORT. & FRANCES COLLINS.
Sweet Anne Page. | Transmigration.
From Midnight to Midnight.
Blacksmith and Scholar.
Village Comedy. | You Play Me False.

By Mrs. H. LOVETT CAMERON.
Juliet's Guardian. | Deceivers Ever.

By WILKIE COLLINS.
Armadale.
After Dark.
No Name.
Antonina. | Basil.
Hide and Seek.
The Dead Secret.
Queen of Hearts.
My Miscellanies.
Woman in White.
The Moonstone.
Man and Wife.
Poor Miss Finch.
Miss or Mrs?
New Magdalen.
The Frozen Deep.
The Two Destinies.
Law and the Lady.
Haunted Hotel.
The Fallen Leaves.
Jezebel's Daughter.
The Black Robe.
Heart and Science.
"I Say No."
Little Novels.
The Evil Genius.
The Legacy of Cain
A Rogue's Life.
Blind Love.

By DUTTON COOK.
Paul Foster's Daughter.

By WILLIAM CYPLES.
Hearts of Gold.

By ALPHONSE DAUDET.
The Evangelist; or, Port Salvation.

By JAMES DE MILLE.
A Castle in Spain.

By J. LEITH DERWENT.
Our Lady of Tears. | Circe's Lovers.

By Mrs. ANNIE EDWARDES.
Archie Lovell.

By PERCY FITZGERALD.
Fatal Zero.

By R. E. FRANCILLON.
Queen Cophetua. | A Real Queen.
One by One. | King or Knave?

Pref. by Sir BARTLE FRERE.
Pandurang Hari.

By EDWARD GARRETT.
The Capel Girls.

THE PICCADILLY (3/6) NOVELS—*continued.*

By CHARLES GIBBON.
Robin Gray. | The Golden Shaft.
In Honour Bound. | Of High Degree.
Loving a Dream.
The Flower of the Forest.

By JULIAN HAWTHORNE.
Garth. | Dust.
Ellice Quentin. | Fortune's Fool.
Sebastian Strome. | Beatrix Randolph.
David Poindexter's Disappearance.
The Spectre of the Camera.

By Sir A. HELPS.
Ivan de Biron.

By ISAAC HENDERSON.
Agatha Page.

By Mrs. ALFRED HUNT.
The Leaden Casket. | Self-Condemned.
That other Person.

By JEAN INGELOW.
Fated to be Free.

By R. ASHE KING.
A Drawn Game.
"The Wearing of the Green."

By HENRY KINGSLEY.
Number Seventeen.

By E. LYNN LINTON.
Patricia Kemball. | Ione.
Under which Lord? | Paston Carew.
"My Love!" | Sowing the Wind.
The Atonement of Leam Dundas.
The World Well Lost.

By HENRY W. LUCY.
Gideon Fleyce.

By JUSTIN McCARTHY.
A Fair Saxon. | Donna Quixote.
Linley Rochford. | Maid of Athens.
Miss Misanthrope. | Camiola.
The Waterdale Neighbours.
My Enemy's Daughter.
Dear Lady Disdain.
The Comet of a Season.

By AGNES MACDONELL.
Quaker Cousins.

By FLORENCE MARRYAT.
Open! Sesame!

By D. CHRISTIE MURRAY.
Life's Atonement. | Coals of Fire.
Joseph's Coat. | Val Strange.
A Model Father. | Hearts.
A Bit of Human Nature.
First Person Singular.
Cynic Fortune.
The Way of the World.

By MURRAY & HERMAN.
The Bishops' Bible.

By GEORGES OHNET.
A Weird Gift.

THE PICCADILLY (3/6) NOVELS—*continued.*

By Mrs. OLIPHANT.
Whiteladies.

By OUIDA.
Held in Bondage. | Two Little Wooden
Strathmore. | Shoes.
Chandos. | In a Winter City.
Under Two Flags. | Ariadne.
Idalia. | Friendship.
CecilCastlemaine's | Moths. | Ruffino.
Gage. | Pipistrello.
Tricotrin. | Puck. | A Village Commune
Folle Farine. | Bimbi. | Wanda.
A Dog of Flanders. | Frescoes.
Pascarel. | Signa. | In Maremma.
Princess Naprax- | Othmar. | Syrlin.
ine. | Guilderoy.

By MARGARET A. PAUL.
Gentle and Simple.

By JAMES PAYN.
Lost Sir Massingberd.
Less Black than We're Painted.
A Confidential Agent.
A Grape from a Thorn.
Some Private Views.
In Peril and Privation.
The Mystery of Mirbridge.
The Canon's Ward.
Walter's Word. | Talk of the Town.
By Proxy. | Holiday Tasks.
High Spirits. | The Burnt Million.
Under One Roof. | The Word and the
From Exile. | Will.
Glow-worm Tales. | Sunny Stories.

By E. C. PRICE.
Valentina. | The Foreigners.
Mrs. Lancaster's Rival.

By CHARLES READE.
It is Never Too Late to Mend.
The Double Marriage.
Love Me Little, Love Me Long.
The Cloister and the Hearth.
The Course of True Love.
The Autobiography of a Thief.
Put Yourself in his Place.
A Terrible Temptation.
Singleheart and Doubleface.
Good Stories of Men and other Animals.
Hard Cash. | Wandering Heir.
Peg Woffington. | A Woman-Hater.
ChristieJohnstone. | A Simpleton.
Griffith Gaunt. | Readiana.
Foul Play. | The Jilt.

By Mrs. J. H. RIDDELL.
Her Mother's Darling.
Prince of Wales's Garden Party.
Weird Stories.

By F. W. ROBINSON.
Women are Strange.
The Hands of Justice.

By W. CLARK RUSSELL.
An Ocean Tragedy.
My Shipmate Louise.

By JOHN SAUNDERS.
Guy Waterman. | Two Dreamers.
Bound to the Wheel.
The Lion in the Path.

CHATTO & WINDUS, 214, PICCADILLY. 29

THE PICCADILLY (3/6) NOVELS—*continued*.

By KATHARINE SAUNDERS.
Margaret and Elizabeth.
Gideon's Rock. | Heart Salvage.
The High Mills. | Sebastian.

By HAWLEY SMART.
Without Love or Licence.

By R. A. STERNDALE.
The Afghan Knife.

By BERTHA THOMAS.
Proud Maisie. | Cressida.
The Violin-player.

By FRANCES E. TROLLOPE.
Like Ships upon the Sea.
Anne Furness. | Mabel's Progress.

THE PICCADILLY (3/6) NOVELS—*continued*.

By ANTHONY TROLLOPE.
Frau Frohmann. | Kept in the Dark.
Marion Fay. | Land-Leaguers.
The Way We Live Now.
Mr. Scarborough's Family.

By IVAN TURGENIEFF &c.
Stories from Foreign Novelists.

By C. C. FRASER-TYTLER.
Mistress Judith.

By SARAH TYTLER.
The Bride's Pass. | Lady Bell.
Noblesse Oblige. | Buried Diamonds.
The Blackhall Ghosts.

CHEAP EDITIONS OF POPULAR NOVELS.
Post 8vo, illustrated boards, 2s. each.

By ARTEMUS WARD.
Artemus Ward Complete.

By EDMOND ABOUT.
The Fellah.

By HAMILTON AIDE.
Carr of Carrlyon. | Confidences.

By MARY ALBERT.
Brooke Finchley's Daughter.

By Mrs. ALEXANDER.
Maid, Wife, or Widow? | Valerie's Fate.

By GRANT ALLEN.
Strange Stories. | The Devil's Die.
Philistia. | This Mortal Coil.
Babylon. | In all Shades.
The Beckoning Hand.
For Maimie's Sake. | Tents of Shem.

By ALAN ST. AUBYN.
A Fellow of Trinity.

By Rev. S. BARING GOULD.
Red Spider. | Eve.

By FRANK BARRETT.
Fettered for Life.
Between Life and Death.

By SHELSLEY BEAUCHAMP.
Grantley Grange.

By W. BESANT & J. RICE.
This Son of Vulcan. | By Celia's Arbour.
My Little Girl. | Monks of Thelema.
Case of Mr. Lucraft. | The Seamy Side.
Golden Butterfly. | Ten Years' Tenant.
Ready-Money Mortiboy.
With Harp and Crown.
'Twas in Trafalgar's Bay.
The Chaplain of the Fleet.

By WALTER BESANT.
Dorothy Forster. | Uncle Jack.
Children of Gibeon. | Herr Paulus.
All Sorts and Conditions of Men.
The Captains' Room.
All in a Garden Fair.
The World Went Very Well Then.
For Faith and Freedom.

By FREDERICK BOYLE.
Camp Notes. | Savage Life.
Chronicles of No-man's Land.

By BRET HARTE.
Flip. | Californian Stories
Maruja. | Gabriel Conroy.
An Heiress of Red Dog.
The Luck of Roaring Camp.
A Phyllis of the Sierras.

By HAROLD BRYDGES.
Uncle Sam at Home.

By ROBERT BUCHANAN.
The Shadow of the | The Martyrdom of
Sword. | Madeline.
A Child of Nature. | Annan Water.
God and the Man. | The New Abelard.
Love Me for Ever. | Matt.
Foxglove Manor. | The Heir of Linne.
The Master of the Mine.

By HALL CAINE.
The Shadow of a Crime.
A Son of Hagar. | The Deemster.

By Commander CAMERON.
The Cruise of the "Black Prince."

By Mrs. LOVETT CAMERON
Deceivers Ever. | Juliet's Guardian

By AUSTIN CLARE.
For the Love of a Lass.

By Mrs. ARCHER CLIVE.
Paul Ferroll.
Why Paul Ferroll Killed his Wife.

By MACLAREN COBBAN.
The Cure of Souls.

By C. ALLSTON COLLINS.
The Bar Sinister.

MORT. & FRANCES COLLINS
Sweet Anne Page. | Transmigration.
From Midnight to Midnight.
A Fight with Fortune.
Sweet and Twenty. | Village Comedy.
Frances. | You Play me False.
Blacksmith and Scholar.

BOOKS PUBLISHED BY

Two-Shilling Novels—*continued.*

By WILKIE COLLINS.
Armadale.
After Dark.
No Name.
Antonina. | Basil.
Hide and Seek.
The Dead Secret.
Queen of Hearts.
Miss or Mrs?
New Magdalen.
The Frozen Deep.
Law and the Lady.
The Two Destinies.
Haunted Hotel.
A Rogue's Life.
My Miscellanies.
Woman in White.
The Moonstone.
Man and Wife.
Poor Miss Finch.
The Fallen Leaves.
Jezebel's Daughter
The Black Robe.
Heart and Science.
"I Say No."
The Evil Genius.
Little Novels.
Legacy of Cain.
Blind Love.

By M. J. COLQUHOUN.
Every Inch a Soldier.

By DUTTON COOK.
Leo. | Paul Foster's Daughter.

By C. EGBERT CRADDOCK.
Prophet of the Great Smoky Mountains.

By WILLIAM CYPLES.
Hearts of Gold.

By ALPHONSE DAUDET.
The Evangelist; or, Port Salvation.

By JAMES DE MILLE.
A Castle in Spain.

By J. LEITH DERWENT.
Our Lady of Tears. | Circe's Lovers.

By CHARLES DICKENS.
Sketches by Boz. | Oliver Twist.
Pickwick Papers. | Nicholas Nickleby.

By DICK DONOVAN.
The Man-Hunter. | Caught at Last!
Tracked and Taken.
Who Poisoned Hetty Duncan?
The Man from Manchester.
A Detective's Triumphs.

By CONAN DOYLE, &c.
Strange Secrets.

By Mrs. ANNIE EDWARDES.
A Point of Honour. | Archie Lovell.

By M. BETHAM-EDWARDS.
Felicia. | Kitty.

By EDWARD EGGLESTON.
Roxy.

By PERCY FITZGERALD.
Bella Donna.
Never Forgotten.
The Second Mrs. Tillotson.
Seventy-five Brooke Street.
The Lady of Brantome.
Polly.
Fatal Zero.

ALBANY DE FONBLANQUE.
Filthy Lucre.

By R. E. FRANCILLON.
Olympia.
One by One.
A Real Queen.
Queen Cophetua.
King or Knave?
Romances of Law.

By HAROLD FREDERICK.
Seth's Brother's Wife.
The Lawton Girl.

Pref. by Sir BARTLE FRERE.
Pandurang Hari.

Two-Shilling Novels—*continued.*

By HAIN FRISWELL.
One of Two.

By EDWARD GARRETT.
The Capel Girls.

By CHARLES GIBBON.
Robin Gray.
Fancy Free.
For Lack of Gold.
What will the World Say?
In Love and War.
For the King.
In Pastures Green.
Queen of Meadow.
A Heart's Problem.
The Dead Heart.
In Honour Bound.
Flower of Forest.
Braes of Yarrow.
The Golden Shaft.
Of High Degree.
Mead and Stream.
Loving a Dream.
A Hard Knot.
Heart's Delight.
Blood-Money.

By WILLIAM GILBERT.
Dr. Austin's Guests. | James Duke.
The Wizard of the Mountain.

By HENRY GREVILLE.
A Noble Woman.

By JOHN HABBERTON.
Brueton's Bayou. | Country Luck.

By ANDREW HALLIDAY.
Every-Day Papers.

By Lady DUFFUS HARDY.
Paul Wynter's Sacrifice.

By THOMAS HARDY.
Under the Greenwood Tree.

By J. BERWICK HARWOOD.
The Tenth Earl.

By JULIAN HAWTHORNE.
Garth.
Ellice Quentin.
Fortune's Fool.
Miss Cadogna.
David Poindexter's Disappearance.
The Spectre of the Camera.
Sebastian Strome.
Dust.
Beatrix Randolph.
Love—or a Name.

By Sir ARTHUR HELPS.
Ivan de Biron.

By Mrs. CASHEL HOEY.
The Lover's Creed.

By Mrs. GEORGE HOOPER.
The House of Raby.

By TIGHE HOPKINS.
'Twixt Love and Duty.

By Mrs. ALFRED HUNT.
Thornicroft's Model. | Self Condemned.
That Other Person. | Leaden Casket.

By JEAN INGELOW.
Fated to be Free.

By HARRIETT JAY.
The Dark Colleen.
The Queen of Connaught.

By MARK KERSHAW.
Colonial Facts and Fictions.

By R. ASHE KING.
A Drawn Game. | Passion's Slave.
"The Wearing of the Green."

Two-Shilling Novels—*continued.*

By HENRY KINGSLEY.
Oakshott Castle.

By JOHN LEYS.
The Lindsays.

By MARY LINSKILL.
In Exchange for a Soul.

By E. LYNN LINTON.
Patricia Kemball. | Paston Carew.
World Well Lost. | "My Love!"
Under which Lord? | Ione.
The Atonement of Leam Dundas.
With a Silken Thread.
The Rebel of the Family.
Sowing the Wind.

By HENRY W. LUCY.
Gideon Fleyce.

By JUSTIN McCARTHY.
A Fair Saxon. | Donna Quixote.
Linley Rochford. | Maid of Athens.
Miss Misanthrope. | Camiola.
Dear Lady Disdain.
The Waterdale Neighbours.
My Enemy's Daughter.
The Comet of a Season.

By AGNES MACDONELL.
Quaker Cousins.

KATHARINE S. MACQUOID.
The Evil Eye. | Lost Rose.

By W. H. MALLOCK.
The New Republic.

By FLORENCE MARRYAT.
Open! Sesame! | Fighting the Air
A Harvest of Wild Oats.
Written in Fire.

By J. MASTERMAN
Half-a-dozen Daughters.

By BRANDER MATTHEWS.
A Secret of the Sea.

By JEAN MIDDLEMASS.
Touch and Go. | Mr. Dorillion.

By Mrs. MOLESWORTH.
Hathercourt Rectory.

By J. E. MUDDOCK.
Stories Weird and Wonderful.
The Dead Man's Secret.

By D. CHRISTIE MURRAY.
A Model Father. | Old Blazer's Hero.
Joseph's Coat. | Hearts.
Coals of Fire. | Way of the World.
Val Strange. | Cynic Fortune.
A Life's Atonement.
By the Gate of the Sea.
A Bit of Human Nature.
First Person Singular.

By MURRAY and HERMAN.
One Traveller Returns.
Paul Jones's Alias.

By HENRY MURRAY.
A Game of Bluff.

By ALICE O'HANLON.
The Unforeseen. | Chance? or Fate?

Two-Shilling Novels—*continued.*

By GEORGES OHNET.
Doctor Rameau. | A Last Love.

By Mrs. OLIPHANT.
Whiteladies. | The Primrose Path.
The Greatest Heiress in England.

By Mrs. ROBERT O'REILLY.
Phœbe's Fortunes.

By OUIDA.
Held in Bondage. | Two Little Wooden
Strathmore. | Shoes.
Chandos. | Ariadne.
Under Two Flags. | Friendship.
Idalia. | Moths.
CecilCastlemaine's | Pipistrello.
 Gage. | A Village Com-
Tricotrin. | mune.
Puck. | Bimbi.
Folle Farine. | Wanda.
A Dog of Flanders. | Frescoes.
Pascarel. | In Maremma.
Signa. | Othmar.
Princess Naprax- | Guilderoy.
 ine. | Ouida's Wisdom,
In a Winter City. | Wit, and Pathos.

MARGARET AGNES PAUL.
Gentle and Simple.

By JAMES PAYN.
Bentinck's Tutor. | £200 Reward.
Murphy's Master. | Marine Residence.
A County Family. | Mirk Abbey.
At Her Mercy. | By Proxy.
Cecil's Tryst. | Under One Roof.
Clyffards of Clyffe. | High Spirits.
Foster Brothers. | Carlyon's Year.
Found Dead. | From Exile.
Best of Husbands. | For Cash Only.
Walter's Word. | Kit.
Halves. | The Canon's Ward
Fallen Fortunes. | Talk of the Town.
Humorous Stories. | Holiday Tasks.
Lost Sir Massingberd.
A Perfect Treasure.
A Woman's Vengeance.
The Family Scapegrace.
What He Cost Her.
Gwendoline's Harvest.
Like Father, Like Son.
Married Beneath Him.
Not Wooed, but Won.
Less Black than We're Painted.
A Confidential Agent.
Some Private Views.
A Grape from a Thorn.
Glow-worm Tales.
The Mystery of Mirbridge.

By C. L. PIRKIS.
Lady Lovelace.

By EDGAR A. POE.
The Mystery of Marie Roget.

By E. C. PRICE.
Valentina. | The Foreigners.
Mrs. Lancaster's Rival.
Gerald.

TWO-SHILLING NOVELS—*continued*.

By CHARLES READE.
It is Never Too Late to Mend.
Christie Johnstone.
Put Yourself in His Place.
The Double Marriage.
Love Me Little, Love Me Long.
The Cloister and the Hearth.
The Course of True Love.
Autobiography of a Thief.
A Terrible Temptation.
The Wandering Heir.
Singleheart and Doubleface.
Good Stories of Men and other Animals.
Hard Cash. | A Simpleton.
Peg Woffington. | Readiana.
Griffith Gaunt. | A Woman-Hater.
Foul Play. | The Jilt.

By Mrs. J. H. RIDDELL.
Weird Stories. | Fairy Water.
Her Mother's Darling.
Prince of Wales's Garden Party.
The Uninhabited House.
The Mystery in Palace Gardens.

By F. W. ROBINSON.
Women are Strange.
The Hands of Justice.

By JAMES RUNCIMAN.
Skippers and Shellbacks.
Grace Balmaign's Sweetheart.
Schools and Scholars.

By W. CLARK RUSSELL.
Round the Galley Fire.
On the Fo'k'sle Head.
In the Middle Watch.
A Voyage to the Cape.
A Book for the Hammock.
The Mystery of the "Ocean Star."
The Romance of Jenny Harlowe.
An Ocean Tragedy.

GEORGE AUGUSTUS SALA.
Gaslight and Daylight.

By JOHN SAUNDERS.
Guy Waterman. | Two Dreamers.
The Lion in the Path.

By KATHARINE SAUNDERS.
Joan Merryweather. | Heart Salvage.
The High Mills. | Sebastian.
Margaret and Elizabeth.

By GEORGE R. SIMS.
Rogues and Vagabonds.
The Ring o' Bells.
Mary Jane's Memoirs.
Mary Jane Married.
Tales of To-day. | Dramas of Life.
Tinkletop's Crime.

By ARTHUR SKETCHLEY.
A Match in the Dark.

By T. W. SPEIGHT.
The Mysteries of Heron Dyke.
The Golden Hoop. | By Devious Ways.
Hoodwinked, &c.

TWO-SHILLING NOVELS—*continued*.

By R. A. STERNDALE.
The Afghan Knife.

By R. LOUIS STEVENSON.
New Arabian Nights. | Prince Otto.

BY BERTHA THOMAS.
Cressida. | Proud Maisie.
The Violin-player.

By WALTER THORNBURY.
Tales for the Marines.
Old Stories Re-told.

T. ADOLPHUS TROLLOPE.
Diamond Cut Diamond.

By F. ELEANOR TROLLOPE.
Like Ships upon the Sea.
Anne Furness. | Mabel's Progress.

By ANTHONY TROLLOPE.
Frau Frohmann. | Kept in the Dark.
Marion Fay. | John Caldigate.
The Way We Live Now.
The American Senator.
Mr. Scarborough's Family.
The Land-Leaguers.
The Golden Lion of Granpere.

By J. T. TROWBRIDGE.
Farnell's Folly.

By IVAN TURGENIEFF, &c.
Stories from Foreign Novelists.

By MARK TWAIN.
Tom Sawyer. | A Tramp Abroad.
The Stolen White Elephant.
A Pleasure Trip on the Continent.
Huckleberry Finn.
Life on the Mississippi.
The Prince and the Pauper.

By C. C. FRASER-TYTLER.
Mistress Judith.

By SARAH TYTLER.
The Bride's Pass. | Noblesse Oblige.
Buried Diamonds. | Disappeared.
Saint Mungo's City. | Huguenot Family.
Lady Bell. | Blackhall Ghosts.
What She Came Through.
Beauty and the Beast.
Citoyenne Jaqueline.

By J. S. WINTER.
Cavalry Life. | Regimental Legends.

By H. F. WOOD.
The Passenger from Scotland Yard.
The Englishman of the Rue Cain.

By Lady WOOD.
Sabina.

CELIA PARKER WOOLLEY.
Rachel Armstrong; or, Love & Theology

By EDMUND YATES.
The Forlorn Hope. | Land at Last.
Castaway.

OGDEN, SMALE AND CO. LIMITED, PRINTERS, GREAT SAFFRON HILL, E.C.

www.ingramcontent.com/pod-product-compliance
Lightning Source LLC
Chambersburg PA
CBHW032052220426
43664CB00008B/975